I0528953

ALL IN ONE MYSTERY

KEITH PAUL PHILLIP

All in one mystery
Copyright © 2024 by Keith Paul Phillip

ISBN: 978-1962497930(sc)

ISBN: 978-1962497947(e)

All rights reserved. No part of this publication may be reproduced, distributed, or transmitted in any form or by any means, including photocopying, recording, or other electronic or mechanical methods, without the prior written permission of the publisher and/or the author, except in the case of brief quotations embodied in critical reviews and other noncommercial uses permitted by copyright law.

The views expressed in this book are solely those of the author and do not necessarily reflect the views of the publisher, and the publisher hereby disclaims any responsibility for them.

The Reading Glass Books
1-888-420-3050
www.readingglassbooks.com
fulfillment@readingglassbooks.com

TABLE OF CONTENTS

I AM, THE BLACK CHILD

LOOK NOT UPON ME, I AM THE BLACK child, like a Lilly among thorns as the apple tree among the trees of the woods. Like a cosmic flame of reality like a natural force of nature. I have my stories to tell.

Pleasant and kind, black, powerful, beauty fears no foes.

I am the black child, one with, positive, character adding to my mental capacity with moral values and Maximum principles as a particular individual, I have my story to tell. As I rise as a black man ain't no doubt about it, it's a big risk to my life. I am willing to take the risk is JAH, who rules the universe I am willing to stand by the word if each of us has to go to our grave maybe this is how I was meant to die., then so be it.

I am the black child, there's a bounty on my head a warrant out for me. I haven't done anything wrong but I am a fugitive, I have my story to tell. The system, have dug out a pit they fill in it. I have learned many lessons they need utmost respect it's a means to an end but the facts remain the same. I don't care what you think about me I shall not quit, I have the identity that you need you think you have all the answers.

I am the black child, this is my favorite story to tell. One life, only one life I need, one life for me, that's all I need and that's the life I love. You can't change my history, you can't change my official culture. Sorry for me, feel sorry for yourself, sorry for the pain, sorry for the wrong things you continue to do. My life is full of wonder, look not upon me, I am the black man.

A WOMAN IS A NEED.

SHE'S THE QUEEN OF THE UNIVERSE, ONE OF virtue one of grace. A woman is a need, as a child needs its mother, a woman is a need, as the elements of life as the elements of the earth itself is strong. A strong woman is like a staff, one who defines, love, kind, fake proof, peaceful, perfect, her techniques are exceedingly great. She's the backbone of the household. She got to keep up the pace in child Birth without any reproach. I will always recommend her excellence She's unreplaceable She's my hereditary. There are certain parts we all have to play, hers is to the purpose, holding the fort. She's one of perfection, the one who bears our pain who feels our experience the most in life. A mother's love is a force like no other her love is amazing she is the only one who made us stronger. On my honor, I give her my word, independently. It's my official duty. A woman is the daughter of the highest as one who is certainly sure to be always there, a mother is a force of nature as no other in the universe.

TREAT MANKIND A LITTLE KINDLIER

NEVER BE TOO SWIFT TO JUDGMENT, EVIL PREYS on the innocent, abuse is a very bad intent, why follow your own heart. What a man sow he shall reap. Do good to others in the hopes they would do the same, we need to share some love. I am my brother's keeper a fact I won't complicate, we are truly brothers and sisters, let's heal our differences.

I am so tired, it's has become so discomforting to my soul, I need some love to ease the pain. Good luck for yourself and bad to others is such a bad intent without any consideration.

Money and love everyone wants that have needs but everyone doesn't always have, Money or love. Do you want it or did you get it and didn't want it? What you waste today you might just need it tomorrow. Heart to heart, man to man, you better know what you value.

Don't defile love by pretense, love by trustworthiness, and confidence. Now walk through eternity as a good person.

Before I let you go, life is short, understand yourself and treat mankind a little kindlier. The world is very judgmental, according to your works you shall get paid.

4

ONE PROMISE

I HAVE NO AUTHORITY, OR EVER CLAIMED TOO but I pledge these words to be true and proven.

O, death, defeat, or victory one promise we all bound to receive. Watching, waiting, from unknown places bearings witness to the purpose we serve.

The gift of life is the focus. The beauty and mystic of life are blowing everywhere, where do we go from here where did it come from, where did it go. No one knows no one to tell, who knows?

Life, love, light, complete its cycle, over and over again, in such infinite capacities. Peace, perfect, peace, without beginning, without end, just as planned.

Let that beautiful, flame ignite and shine fought, forevermore, let us celebrate its brilliance, eternally. Let joy and perfect harmony be the words of this precious life let it run as the flowing river. Honor me in such spiritual memories, as in my transportation in life as a pose to death, until we meet again, have the courage and be kind.

JUST A LITTLE BIT OF LOVE

A LITTLE BIT OF LOVE WOULD DO JUST fine just a little bit would be enough to turn a little amber into a flame, just a little flutter of love with understanding withstand the test of time could be the greatest love of all. Love controls the light most amazingly if you feel love the sky is no limit just a little bit of love. If this world was mine I would spread love all over the globe to the little boy and girls, teachers us to get the best results. When you give love free from your heart and soul, it feels like 100% heat from the fire, love is in control. Love and understanding, what a huge difference it makes. Collect your thoughts in every country and put a bright smile on your face and turn that flitter into a flame. A little bit of love is a love that I can share it's the magic which it creates. It's so powerful, hypnotic, telepathic, change you with its spells. Love and peace are all we need, it will pick up your trail, near or far away, put your heart together when you are willing to go the extra mile, love is justified. It's either you have love or none at all. We keep searching for perfect love, there's none as simple as to be skin deep. It appears to me, love goes to the bone is the greatest love in the world, a little bit of love is better than no love at all.

A DIFFERENCE IS A DIFFERENCE ONLY WHEN YOU MAKE A DIFFERENCE.

THIS IS INTERESTING, ENVY IS A SYMPTOM of our uniqueness and self-worth but each of us has sometimes to give that no one else possesses. The difference is a difference only when you make a difference.

People who care for you won't ever hurt you but if they do you will see it in their eyes for they would be hurting too. The eyes are the window to the soul. A difference is a difference only when you make it a difference.

False friends are like shadows, keeping close to you when you walk in the sunshine but leaves you as soon as you cross into the shade. A positive attitude may not solve all your problems but it would annoy enough to make it worth the effort. A difference is a difference only when you make it a difference.

The more you accept the more you will be disappointed in life. Faith is taking the first step even when you don't see the whole picture, which sometimes we feel that we should know but Discipline is the bridge between our goals and accomplishments. One of life's greatest secrets is to make stepping-stones out of stumbling blocks. A difference is a difference only when you make it a difference.

Be not be discouraged if you do not succeed the first time, no one ever learns to walk by only taking one step. Learning without reflecting would be a waste of time, reflecting without Learning would be dangerous. A difference is a difference only when you make it a difference.

If you try to keep things in your own hands and don't pass it on, you just might lose it all, but when you share that which you have with mankind you will still possess them in the end. No foe or any situation can defeat you when GOD is on your side if God is for you who can be against us. A difference is a difference only when you make it a difference.

What a man does it's his own affair.

Too often we see it, time and time again, everyone should take responsibility for their actions, in other words to each his own, what a man sow is that he will reap.

Look me straight in the eyes and tell me what you don't understand about, good and bad, right and wrong when you know well it's woven into the fabric of our existence and don't necessarily have to be taught.

Nevertheless, it will take a bigger person who is willing to admit, without any denial of any wrongdoing don't matter how humiliating it may feel. Mankind must learn to display the inner discipline required to carry out the appropriate actions which represent, core, values, and principles. His rest shall be comfortable and sweetest nights.

AFRICA.

WE SHINE IN ALL OUR BRILLIANCE ON THIS brand new day, Africa, my love for you and my people, could never fade. Collectively, my people could live without you.

You do more harm than good. Living with you is not living at all.

I could do anything you can do and better, am still going to live the life I love. Allow us to leave in our multitudes and lead the way. Please, what I see makes my heart leap.

We have our priest, prophets, and king, culture, and our spiritual ways of life, don't make any mistakes, we created the alphabet, cosmetics, chemistry, and ideology. We made great contributions to civilization.

All we have contributed are at high risk to be replaced by the craft you created.

Woe unto the man, who takes my home by force, woe be to them like a infectious, disease, polluting our land, that's what at stake. Stealing, stealing, in the name of God, all my life because the doors were opened wide. From that time our rich future was over if I had known their intentions, now am on the ground. Here are the facts, down in the Pitts, forever poor.

Never thought such things were possible, what we know and what we did not know? What we did not understand?

We didn't know the impact it would have today, the whole area, the whole region, continues to get hit hard. You built yourcivilization, structure on top of mines to no cost, absolutely free.

We get no benefit.

We did not complain while our children were caught. Now we know the condition we got too wake up, and reclaim what belongs to us. Am telling you there's no basis for your argument, you got to go stop trying to take my land, it was ours since the beginning.

From, Africa to America, that is it, we won't let anyone else into the country. I document that injustice petty for you, your love has only brought me, war, not happiness, I am reporting this reality, accurately. It's so hard to see what your love means. I can't imagine what my eyes were witnessing, you stole away my joy and happiness, Africa, my heart desire.

I love the land, time, and time again, and everything we set our minds on. I speak out because I don't believe one word you say give me beautiful Africa, all the time, preserving everything, it was the biggest crime in the history of mankind. Talking about the same old story, slavery.

BREATH ON MY OWN CONSCIOUSNESS

IN MY CONSCIOUSNESS, I ATTEMPT TO BREATHE, TAKING a detour from the foundation of the lungs. Taking deep rips, fast, and slow on my own, I found myself gasping for breath it was a difficult thought. I even experimented trying to maintain the rhythm and beat of my heart, that beautiful organ, I have failed after many attempts to do even that on my own consciousness. I am beautifully created, intelligently designed, the omnipresence inside, out. I live a colorful life, super-powerful, life over death. The presence of life could be found everywhere, even in the most inhospitable, remote places. Life is determined to manifest itself, procreating, reproducing, circulating, no one knows how it got started, standing out, and fine turning itself, life is a purpose, or we all will just be in existence, no other reason for being here. Celebrate life, it's an honor, and privilege, man, an entity from a particular order with the essential tool in the servitude of mankind. Art, bring to life a sculptured detail. My life is in the singular, and plural, light, time, and space. Physically, mentally, and spiritually. To the rescue the master in me has awake. Creating, colliding particles, atomic dust, exploding, countless stars around a future will depend on moral success. Around me is an oar, a world, one which tool year in the making, it's a colorful world, doing things in the orderly fashion, has become an incredible way of life to me.

CHRISTMAS IS FOR KIDS

CHRISTMAS IS COMING. LET THEM CELEBRATE IN THE neighborhood, Christmas is for kids. Let naughty or nice not judge them from having fun, being happy, we got to make them happy, give them the best feeling in the world. It's important to kids, they love the Christmas holiday seasons. It's the one day you have to share the love with everyone. Come to my home, I will come to your home, this holiday we will share love and devotion. Mankind will be enjoying the world's celebration. One day we all have been anticipating all year through, looking forward in preparing, gifts for that favorite day of the year, it's the holiday season, winter is already here, Christmas trees is on the way home. Enjoy this season, on this day the son was born. With all the gifts we receive this Christmas holiday this is the greatest gift of them all. Educate children, teach them what this season is all about, and all the little children would have a fun happy holiday. Share the cheer, and smile, participate for the holidays.

O, LOOK

O, LOOK, HURRY FOR NOTHING IS WAITING to happen. More or less play a major role in the communities. O, look, another ghetto child has lost the way, and don't know who to turn to. Which way should they turn, the uneducated can't read-write or spell most likely to fail, join a gang world, pick up the gun, living a life of crime, their future is unknown as he's now a criminal at large. Life is on the hustle, the victims never had any chance, hungry was the cry of the child from the ghetto. The environment is one of despair, defeat, lost dreams, and hopes. Ponder on those on top of the food chain. Life is no easy road. It is what it is, predator, or prey. Love could not be found, incapable of loving someone. It's a jungle, mostly for the child of the ghettos. There is no love, sick and tired of being taken advantage of, special codes, blood in blood out, it's a sad case, where some have succeeded, many have failed. The sun, atomic solar energy, a natural source of light, life, energy every day. The stars up above each day they come out at night to shine, and twinkle over us. The celestial bodies guide us all along the way, you see we can rise together, liberate ourselves, liberate mankind. Right here, now, to live a better life on this planet earth, O, look, hurry for nothing is waiting to happen.

BETTER OURSELVES

LONG LIVE EDUCATION, BUT THERE IS ALWAYS, ways, to improvements, and bettering ourselves, these are the time. You got to keep on trying, self- determination to succeed, ambitiously we could never fail, so a man thinketh so is he. Legacy done laid, and a bright future for the children. Where is your trademark, and signature, designate your own standards. Remember it is not when we expect to live, but how long we can live. As a man thinketh, so is he. If I can do it, who are you, you can do it too, anyone could. It's a long time I have been trying holding on, never giving up the fight, you got to try. No two ways about it, no stepping around. We are the masters of the life we chose to live, all little people have a lot of love to share all those blocked headed people, look what the world has come to, sure, they have a lot, in a safe. So a man thinketh, so is he. We came into this world always meeting others, with respect, and tolerance, those are the ideal, ideas, which we entail, it is the beginning, or is this the end, you have the ability to figure out anything yourself, I have seen them all, none, never, ever, exactly the same. Don't take on the world, never believe, don't let them fool you, read between the lines, uncover what is there. The body is the temple, your mind is the instrument, your physical and spiritual, consciousness, as a man thinketh, so is he.

PROUD PARENT

DON'T LOSE YOUR GROUND, MAKE YOUR PARENTS PROUD, it's our responsibility. To get things done in the proper way, servants would cool your feet but nothing else. My mother and father were good parents they took very good care of me. A happy bread. Fast in the morning, popcorn at the movies. Very optimistic about having fun every day. Hold my hands' mother, no lonely walks in the parks, I love my parent, I do with absolute unconditional, permanent, love. These are real people, the taught me everything I know. Time is the essence, my love is real, I believe what my parent taught me. The family should always stick together. No matter what, under any condition, or circumstances. They say don't take kindness for granted, a kind heart serves a high purpose in our daily lives. Compliment, don't be offensive to anyone. Pay attention, listen, and learn, things of worth, the thing I valued. There's only one truth if we find it, right, and wrong we have serious choices to make, to make some of your life each day. I love my parents, they taught me to love.

CAT, AND MOUSE GAMES

WHAT IS REALLY IMPORTANT IS THE AGE WE are living in, cat, and mouse games, the perfect example, what's going on caught up in a bad situation, making a bad situation worse than it already is. Searching, day time, night time to, no time to lose, I am always on the move. In a rat race. I ain't got no concern for no one, ain't got to shame of nothing at all. I am on the go all day long, I got to get my own. But I picked myself up, came out of the hold on me, took the first step. What's going on? Start to feel the spirit of wisdom in myself, I cried, and cried, for a permanent solution. The sun shall not smite at me by day, or the moon by night, I look to the hills from where cometh my help, my help cometh from the Lord. Ain't nothing out there like what is in me. Nothing that I want to do. It may be a long road ahead, not in the generation in God we trust, I can't take that with me as it's a heck of a ride. For the love of money, is the root of all evil. Pride cometh before a fall, you need a friend more than anything, your family more than anything, if you don't care, it's time to act out or you got to be a lone tree survivor.

READ THE GOOD BOOK

IN FRONT OF YOUR FACE, THEY WOULD STARE in your eyes and smile with you. Behind your back they would laugh at you. What's the use they read the good book, and can't hear a doorman cry, what's the use, where you use to be green, is now dry. Want us to commit a crime. Stand up for the poor, pass it on. Put your bread in the river of love, give thanks you are a fortunate one. Hunger doesn't play, hunger doesn't even have a name or face. Some can't even remember the last time they had something healthy to eat. You knock them down, and they get right back up but hunger won't leave them alone. Put hunger in a box, and lock it up. You have a name everyone knows you by you have a face those who know you, in the dark, sunny, or rain. Hunger doesn't care if people have nothing at all, can't even see a bright shining sun, hunger isn't going anywhere. Life is not right! I have to fight to find some food. While men on earth living like Gods. Look at what they have done, it's repelling, so want to be shall be a hungry man is an angry man, so be it. You better keep an open mind.

IN COEXISTENCE WITH NATURE

IN COEXISTENCE WE COURAGEOUSLY STRUGGLE WITH THE EXISTENCE with nature.

The light was beaming through but the stairs were always there, they never go anywhere at night time like long, couple of hours have passed, it's not artificial, it's a display of nature's magnetic fields, only the conditions are different in the details. The polar lights expand to the equator, like a black ghost moving in the blackness, that is nights. The shining sun disappears, but not for a long time, winter is the season night there are very long, there's no sound, pass hours, why we are who we are is a mystical curiosity, somewhere out there is an interpretation. A figure of light in the bedroom comes through finally, the weather eases, and the moon begins to shine.

LIGHT, DARK, AND A GUILTY CONSCIENCE

YOU SEE, WE ALL WILL AGREE, WE HAVE made some mistakes in our lives before that follows us everywhere we go and is there all the way. What follows us? Light, dark, and a guilty conscience, at the end of the day you will never getaway, you can't run away from yourself. If you never found God inside of you, how could you find God outside of you? Do for me, and I will do for you, and that is today and not tomorrow, don't defile love by pretense, love is there, every time every moment, everywhere in certain ways. Some will admit, love is a mystery the more we distance ourselves from the concept to understand love, love is to learn, and then it comes naturally, but hate is taught. Somedays who can differentiate between, right, and wrong. A home is a place at times the sense of love does cease to exist but could be found far away in distant places.

POEM TO A SONG

WE'RE GOING TO THE PROMISED LAND AND I got a feeling, mysterious feeling, life could change in the blink of the eyes. Life is what you make of it, turn this poem into a song. In case you haven't noticed, in case you haven't heard life is a journey, take care of what you have, and never let it go. Don't let life be a burden to you today, it's just another day if you only let it be, the moment could be life-changing, as easy as, 3,2,1,1,2,3. Stop your negative thinking, and think positive, be constructive, there's no time to waste, no time as the present, do good, and good is sure to follow you, build a world around yourself, just do your best, and you will surely be blessed, and Jah would take care of the rest. What you sow is what you reap, according to your works you shall get pay, do unto others as you would have them do to yourself because what goes up must come down, what goes around comes around again. None shall escape this judgment.

A TIME

I DON'T THINK WHAT THEY ARE SELLING to me seems to add up., I think they would have offered better odds there's a place in my heart where the master lives, there's a reason why man thinks he knows everything. Like a tree in the morning, flourish in the evening, and weathers at night, one a man, and twice a child, a time to live, and a time to die, accepting that, we only live once. Nothing last forever, if we only know the reason why. Everything is for a while when you come to think about it, you can't have everything. Think about the connection, if everyone living knew the secret of life, we would renew life, everlasting, nobody would die that possibility won't ever happen, it doesn't seem to be a reality. That offer could be too extreme, nothing last forever, everything is for a time. There's a reason for life, one more than death for the living. Give a little love, it shall not be in vain, lead the way, show the would you care.

NATURE'S CREATION

COME LET US DISCOVER THE INNER FRONTIERS. Our journey is one of nature's creations come let us discover where do we fit in. It's a modern world, everyone is struggling to enjoy life understanding the knowledge of science, and technology. A molecule, atoms, particles and volcanoes, brain waves, microchips, gravity, and chemistry. It's an extraordinary time we are living in. How do we explain these fantastic technological achievements? Now, are we making any real progress. We have conquered the highest mountains, descent into the deep blue seas, sail the widest oceans, want to know what are those lights in the sky up there, trying to discover outer planetary systems. Dying to dissect the mysteries of the universe. It turns our science, and technology is beautiful, while progress in an unstoppable force but nature knows best in the wonder of the unknown, but we have to go on living the adventure there is never a certainty of what will happen, next.

LIER ON FIRE

I CANNOT BELIEVE IT'S REAL WHEN I THINK about it, it plagues me, blowing my mind, my brains is into pieces. I think I am about to take a three-hour rest. The way in which it will tell a lie, it's a pattern of their behavior. They think they do no harm. They are trying to impress everyone who they could possibly convince. Human contact is to be accepted, to be accepted by the crowds, becoming something much less than human. It's hard to believe, the irony of becoming a liar, building a reputation as a notorious liar. Stop the lying, a liar is a dangerous person, willingly, and knowingly choose to deceive in your daily routine. You intentionally deceiving can cause tragedy. Lying is contrary to the truth and facts. Compounding the truth, fabricating, made up stories, collaborating, most likely to destroy new ties we create becoming enemies, nobody wants to be a friend. Saying one thing, a mean a next, playing games no one could ever pardon, he that tries to hide the truth still does the wrong thing. Speak the truth, tell it like it is, let it will. There's a place where lies originate, you can go there, it's the place for you to go, call hell! Lying is traitor, deadly dangerous, deflecting the truth is becoming impulsive lying is a falsehood, flat out deceiving yourself in any subject of debate. Do not underestimate the power of a lie.

MANKIND

FROM THE TREE OF LIFE, WHO AM I, I am a member of mankind, I manifest, I am a man. So who are you? Are you a member of the biggest conspiracy? The human race who started this conspiracy? Do look, look at us I don't see anything strange here, are we not the same, or do we look different? We share a lot more in common than you may think or do we look alike. Who's comparing anyhow, the same coin has two sides. But if you do think you are somehow better than I am, then we have to find a better way Review or, morals, principles, ethics, values, and behavior, or the truth shall shed its light on every one of your dark tales. Darkness, and light in coexistence, close your eyes, one cannot do without the next. They can't do without each other it's not survival, we all are survivors on this planet earth, one family, mankind, feel the heart beating in your chest, close your eyes again, we are the same. Why on earth we can't live in love, and unity, creating an everlasting and unbreakable bond, let us see what happens. You for me, and I for you, stand up for me, and I will stand for you, let us trust our fellow man, or have you lost your mind. The body is only a vessel for our consciousness. Most people look like most people look past the thing that would matter, maybe the question I should ask, do you trust your fellow man.

HERB

THEY ARE TRYING TO PERSECUTE THE HERB, for what I don't know, with a false allegation, the herd is only natural, let me explain, the herd is good in the morning, it eases the frustration, and pains, what are we so happy about the herb is good for the brain, mane the assessments, and the adjustment, put it into context, put it into proper perspectives, eventually everything will manifest itself. Odds are, it's your many fears, pretty bad numbers, to fail. Stop the hype, and feel the vibes of the good herbs. The main issue, the major factors, is the present, for God's sake, is the examples that we set, actions speak loud, and clear, to know the eyes were meant to see, I know you only believe. The future is in our sight, no surprise, today. It's our zest for life, the herb is very energetic, a pursuit, persistent, one hundred percent, insist on being satisfied. Star bright is the most beautiful way to dazzle, and decorate the mind, and increase your life span as the sun beaming down on the oceans. I am on a campaign trail to legalize the herb; cool heads will prevail.

ARORA

ARCTIC AIR WAS IN SIGHT- UNFOLDING THE BEAUTY of nature polar light expands to the equator like a black ghost moving across the darkness, that is call night. The shining sun disappears, but not for long, winter is the season, nights are very long, you couldn't hear a sound. An hour has passed. Why we are, who we are, living in existence, is a mystical curiosity. We courageously struggle in our existence with nature. Somewhere is an interpretation, figures of light beams through the clouds finally the weather ease, and the moon begins to shine. The stars were always there, they never go anywhere. It's not artificial, it's the display of nature's magnetic field, only the conditions are different in their details. The Arora is beautiful. Northern lights.

WATER

WHEN THE RAIN FALLS, IT'S WINDS, AND COLD high tides, the ocean is choppy and rough. Here comes the rain. The water, on the mountain, the water flowed through the creek and crevasses. Down the sloop to the rivers, springs, and lakes, all of them into one link, all as one they communicate. To utter the word in a form of unknown communicative skills. Evolution, intelligence, spiritually divine, inspired, listen to their words in communication, voices bird's weasels, dog bark, chicken chirps, and tree sweats with winds. As they blow earth, heat, air, and water, you know the parts you play, no limitations, only the potential to open the mind to the constellations of the solar system, moons, and stars. You can't deny that fact. They communicate I know what I am, and what am not. Together we can make it beautiful.

THE TRUTH HURTS

YOU ARE A BIG CORPORATE INVESTOR, BUT your efforts may not be safe as you may think. Nothing hurts like the truth. I know you must be hating me, I don't hate you, I don't need your company. I was never a part of your script. I don't live up to your expectations, my lifestyle is too simple, no interest to you, you have higher standards set, but don't defy my character in comparison to your creed, there's no equal place. I am sorry, boss, I cannot work for you, you can't have it all above everything. When I think about it., you don't care how nobody feeling but yourself. A lack of moral integrity, boss, we are masters of our craft. Boss, you are capable of double standards, that must be immediately addressed. Your life is no better than mines, come down from your prompts, and pride, searching for glory, practice what you preach. Your hypocrisy, it's frightening me, my life is a daily struggle. Now, it's all because of you, I am standing up for myself, I learned my lesson well, you thought me very well, now I am in a situation where I could help others. I cannot trust what you have become too, what you stand for is not able to help others in a similar situation like mines. What you got on me, boss. The memories of you are with one, every breath I take, every beat of my heart, for all things on earth that ever live, and bread, for the world to live in love, forever one dream to come to a reality. Stop the hate, but I am still trying to grasp, the fact, you are cancer to any society, everyone should live the life they choose to live.

PRECONCEPTION

THEY DON'T KNOW, WHAT THEY DON'T KNOW, PRECONCEPTION. We came into life, with a purpose to live, and not to be judge, to be accepted for who you are. It begins when mankind decides to divide themselves into race, man starts with, humiliation, domination, psychological. Wars, crimes, violence, and poverty. It's a terrible sight to witness at this time. The more high-tech machine invented, it's the more efficiently to capable to kill. More people are dying today. Than any other time in history, the smaller the high tech was the more, dangerously efficient it became. More than, one, two, three, four, of my brothers, and sisters, blood is going to spill. They say they want to advance civilization, spilling spaghetti on the wall to see what will stick, failing in every endeavor they attempt. What is required is change, real change that everyone could share. What if someone from ancient time return today, they might say what a mess we made of things, and made some certain recommendation for uniting the earth. The feather, and lead from their highest point, they travel, and land at the same time, a marvel of evolution, nature, and gravity. It's a big difference, mankind is searching to find a way, let's put the pieces together, and build that bridge, by now we should have all the facts we need. These are the actual, root cause, these egos are running a mock. Honoring murderess, as heroes. People may forgive, and forget, but history won't, your word is contrary to images we see. Committing crimes against humanity. Systems are falling apart. Time for a change, we need accountable people, consignor, change, we need people who know better, we need people who care about the beauty of nature. People with discretion, people with consideration.

MAGNET

I SORT AND FIND THIS INFORMATION. MAGNET SOMETIMES attracts, sometimes repels, magnetically charged, but my woman she's so beautiful, this is reality, feeling, this is love it moves me emotionally, like poetry in motion in a world, my world, of meditation, feeling, to communicate to one, and all, universal love, the languages in poetry. In my divine inspiration, I manifest my state of mind, it's a rich quality healthy life, easy die, in life, the vessel is a container for the abundance of running spring water. A spring of fresh start, new beginnings. Life in the immediate, the ultimate experience is in the future, of time, seasons, and the changes, conflict, in their illusions, in a world of chaos, and mayhem, my love I love you as I love poetry, there's nothing as individual as you are. Every woman has something unique about themselves, my woman is like warm spring water, my woman feels so good, she feels alright, and she let it show. The feeling is mutual and I let it show, there's no one like her, no other one for me, her voice, personality, this is how I know my woman loves me, I will never let her down.

LOVE ME

THIS IS WHEN MY HAPPINESS BEGINS 4 AM she wakes up each morning, and before she heads out this door, to work, her lips meet mines with a kiss as I head to the table, she leaves little notes laying on the dinner table saying, I love you, I will give my love to only you, this is how love supposed to be. I can't do without you in my life baby, I need your love, I won't let you go, won't ever say goodbye. I know I love her to., her spirit is free, no pressure is around her, she's not a prisoner, there's no competition when she wants my loving am here when she needs me, I will be there, to keep her happy, and secure, I will never give up on her love, anyway, she's here to stay, because of our history, I love her the same she gives her love to only me, I give my love to only her, baby, I will give my love to you alone, only you. Never found what I was looking for, but I found something, I have lost. Nothing is standing in my way, fool rush in where wise men never dare. What would you do for love, you never miss something until it's gone. you never should appreciate driving you the way people fall in love. Love is something money can't buy. Love is the balance of our emotions it's not a physical, attraction, hurting each other, infatuated if you stay, momentary gratification if you go. Never found what I was looking for but I found something I had lost, I love you then, I love you now, I love you still, I will always love you, I have always, love you.

A GREAT ONE

THE VALUE OF A PERSON, WITH SUBSTANCE, a person means a lot, a person the world can't do without, a great one an entrust is there any pressure? I am the end of your search, the alpha one, if one is a lonely number, one stands alone. That means love is strong I am the one, ready to take on the world, under the star above, shining bright. It's a defying movement in my life., one can make a big difference quantum leaps, so let this battle begin, I call on the leaders of the past, present, future, and beyond, their voices will be heard echoing loudly, it's a cardinal rule blowing in the winds. We gain experience through our daily struggles. Through our cups are dry empty, it's alright, the blurs seem to be clearer now. The same thing you denied us, is the same thing which would unite us as one. What you have to offer are those foolish games you play in. Hypocrites, can't take one for a ride, with your tricks you want to take a bite. When brothers were few where were you? sitting around, while all that life has to offer is there for the taking. My work here is almost over, and done, behind every dark cloud there's a silver line. There's no time like the present, help yourself be an independent man. The river keeps on flowing it's going to be better than you ever thought it would, all road ahead, take the lead, come across, know you can do it, just give all you have to give, pick up yourself, clear your thoughts, be a part of the solution, don't be a problem. Make the right decisions, give it your everything. Move it, get it, everything is visible, victory is yours, thank you very much.

WASTED TALENT

BE AMBITIOUS, PASSIONATE, DRIVEN. START SMALL, BIG VISIONS. If the birds are not content with where they are, why should you be? One of the saddest things in life is wasted talent. Don't be a victim of your circumstances. If it's something you believe in, and it is worth accomplishing the harder you work, at your craft it proves your chance in succeeding looks certainly excellent, I am counting on you. You have no one to depend on but a human error yourself. There are no lazy people only those who are afraid to fail, discipline a bridge between our goals, and accomplishments. Perseverance is a winner of both time, and chance, it's not everyday opportunities that are going to come your way. If I could I would take you there. Hope you are ready when that window opens up and presents itself. Don't be afraid, with confidence. You have already gained the victory, anything is possible. You could turn a minus into a plus, we have done more with less, all you got to do is just try. Opportunity is that special place with that great privilege comes to a greater responsibility with the scope of acting in the role encompassing the obligation of accomplishment. You don't have to forge me, I got to be there, you don't have to twist my arms. I am going to make it. Lifting myself by my on boots straps.

WRITE ABOUT LOVE

SWORD OF COPPER, SWORD OF LIGHTS, BULLETS, GUNS, bombs, crimes, people killing people, no not here today. I don't care. To lead is not to dominate, stop study war. The pen is a mighty powerful instrument. Stop studying too kill. There's no bombs, but the intelligence behind coding the pen shall make sure here's no bombs. You could choose any topic, concept, version, original, or cops. Write about love let's bring love out from the depths of your hearts, like the lights from above. Strong love, love is stronger than war, super powerful love. I want to know this reason why. So I could bring love to the whole world. I will write the report, write the essay, share the information with every man, woman, and child. Good news is here to stay, the velocity is high at this level time is only a concept of human perception, this civilization must be free, liberated, from all from of superstitions, and negativity. Can't we do it tomorrow? I don't think so, leadership takes bomb responsibility. With wars, and rumors of wars, a nation fighting against nations light against darkens, right, against wrong, righteous, against evil. Let us investigate this from the highest level to proclaim love is the highest level of event that we could try to save what little pride we have remained as mankind, past, present, and future, we got to protect love by all means necessary, love is strong than war.

TARGET

DO YOU HAVE IDEAS; I WILL LIKE to listen to what you have to say. They are talking, running their mouths. They don't know what they are talking about, babbling, contriving themselves. Coming up you were their favorite target. Your attention span is as short as your perception of things, and time, and that should be a critical reason to turn around your way of thing. Hemorrhage iron the brain can't wait for you to change your style. It just happens you could turn out to be one of the greatest minds of our time. It could be one of your biggest trip ever. For peace, sake give back to mankind. Give a reason for being a part of this universe. Don't give up your mental capacity to think things out for yourself, and answers your question. I don't matter what part of the world you may be, you must revise who you are, and make your life, and another better, do it for your country, accomplish something we will love.

MOTHER

MOTHER, LET ME TELL YOU ABOUT A MOTHER, when I think about a mother, this is what comes to my mind. My first word was mama. Am mother's love is all the love I needed. All other love are short-range comfort, here's are justified, permanently. Every child needs its mother, she's a giant in their world. What she thought is strict discipline, and manner social skills, I still find healthy useful to me today, her voice was heard. It would grieve me, it won't justify her stature and legacy. A mother story must be told, there no other like her in this world with a heart like hers. Let me tell you about a mother, sit with me, allow me to choose carefully, sensible words, as I indulge myself in this moment of love to express myself to you. Most young people have little skill in reason, wisdom, knowledge, and understanding, a mother's love is a jewel a love from God's firm, knowledge, wisdom, and understanding, a mother rises early to teach her household. with a pleasant smile, kind face, by principle, her examples lead. A mother is the greatest jewel any child could ask for no mother could ever be replaced, children need a mother's love, always, mom. I am proud, I could always depend on your love. A mother will never, ever let you down, a mother's love is the kind of love I need, my mother, no other woman would star up to her.

WOULDN'T IGNORE HER BEAUTY

IT'S NOT EVERYDAY MIRACLES HAPPENS; MY EYES COULD not ignore the beauty it beholds. I saw her dark skin. Her dress was in mile rose colors. I approached her, her eyes matched the colors of her dress, wearing a cool smile that made her face shine glow. That evening, she made it look glamorous, she's a queen, the black woman. Your mother bared you she bought you that bare you. Setting a seal of her heart, and you wear it on your arms, her love is strong, jealousy, cruel, your love is like fire, and overwhelming heat, she's a queen the black woman. She's built as a tower, the favor was found in her eyes, she was quickly spoken for a wall was around her like a palace made out of marble with doors of cedar. Give her riches for water cannot quench her thirst, her continence is excellent, she's one of a kind, she's a queen, the black woman doesn't awake her love, stir up until she was pleased, the words from her lips are friendly and sweet. Turn your eyes away from her before they overcome you. she's the only one, she's on of choice, she's a queen, the black woman.

HUNGER

CHILDREN HUNGRY, WOMAN HUNGRY, BROTHER, AND SISTER TOO. Living in an age of binary codes. Characters zeros and ones. What I am trying to convey, so many things, what more they want from us. What about education, food, clothes, and shelter. Everything is numbered, nothing is affordable. What about our basic, fundamentals, civil rights? What about an honest day work, for an honest day to pay. From the sweat of the brow, man shall eat bread. There is a fire, dust, the universe is screaming, chaos, blood, death, was everywhere, can't even meet my needs. Nothing from nothing leaves nothing. Every day I got to provide for the family. I don't want to beg, I don't want to steal, I don't use profanity, cigarettes kill, alcohol is for a fool. Give me food, give me, food will nourish, and bring good health to my family. I don't want my belly to pain, I don't want any headaches. Give me food right now, today. Watching you through the ages, we are only a product, a commodity, they say nothing ventured nothing gain. I need to provide for my family.

GOD DON'T OWE ME A THING

STAR OF DESTINY, A STAR SO BRIGHT, THIS IS THE AGE, THIS is the time, uncontainable, but contained. The excellence of your power guide, and protect my temple. From sin, you know my deeps. Tomorrow, how could it be, where would you be if you are afraid? God doesn't owe me a thing but my acceptance is guaranteed you got to prove to me this is not reality. There is no lack of patient. Time is insignificant, where there is passion rejoice for the gift of life this day, if you are one with us, don't hate, and grudge, condemning yourself by your judge. How are you having all the answer, love your brother as you love yourself, swinging in your folly, only truth, and right will solve the problems, who have an ear let them hear, who has eyes to see let them see, glorying simplicity, a man is just a man, I don't see anything different from anyone, I have no doubts about my position. Love this time, before good friends turn into enemies. Yesterday is gone, tomorrow is far, far away, all we got is today.

IT HAS A GIFT TO IT

ANOTHER PIECE OF AMBITIOUS WORKS, THE SUN IS setting, the time has taken years on history, and oppression. Through the lives of my brothers, and sisters, telling their stories of the aching, sad, beautiful range of human emotion. The experience is on an intimate scale, which brings my emotion to reality. It has a gift to it, adding sheets of history, with the spirit that narrates the human family living in a vivid, and compelling eye on daily life. Grasping on the dimmest ray of hope, and resilience in a world where there is a constant struggle for survival. This poetry will skillfully tell the human story in an infinite patient vision, the lines are powerful, beautiful, illicit truth that makes the heart dump, and ache, stomach pain, with the ability to portray the full range of our human emotions.

ONE LIGHT

THE SUN SHINES IT'S LIGHT, ONE LIGHT FOR everything, without its energy we will freeze to death school days was really happy, happy, day. You all need an education. It's very important, it's an important tool in the means in this world today. But remember there is a particular attribute we inherited from the very day of our birth conception. Everyone has it, we were given that light from the sun within. The fabric of our existence, first, there is love, and compassion, commonsense, and inspiration, third eye, talent, and skills, creativity, with natural intelligence. To prophecy, the spark. Your mind is the instrument, you are the masters of your craft, the possibilities are endless. Just put your heart into it, work hard with that burning desire in your soul. The secrets of the success behind the seen flow unnoticed. Your absolute discipline will bring about the desired results of your ventures, aim, and objective one hundred percent. It's a given, and take the world you could lend a lot of hope in fostering the joy in the desire to achieve. Consciously, make no mistake incredible, you possess something that could take you where ever you want to go. Around the world, to the moon, and stars above. It's not luck, and chance, science or magnet, believe me, it's not a dream.

CONVERSATIONS WITH MYSELF

I LOVE WALKING, SOMETIMES WHEN I WALK, I hold conversations with myself. I love walking, moving forward. Wise at heart, I have got a mine of my own. It's either you do, or you don't. I could catch all my emotions, happiness, sadness, crying, anger, you want to walk with me. Let's walk my brother, we are brothers, let's walk my sister, we are sisters. Once that was all that mattered, it was none negotiable, I love to walk, let's walk, the truth is self- explanatory, facts merit legitimacy. To visit above, and beyond, that's what we do with questions besides asking them, I did my extensive research, and this is my findings, all their news was meant to scare. Hiding behind the shadows of fear, the truth is what we must bring out on time, that which must come out in the open. You silence, your fear, is a scary story. Should you ever be forced to speak out don't be afraid to its good reason for the wise at heart. Knowledge to keep us safe, and sound. Born to lead. Lead, move forward. Walk vertically, walk upright. You leave me no other choice; our brain is a very powerful tool that has been misunderstood. I love walking, it's an amazing journey.

I WONDER

I WONDER IF WE ARE GIVING UP ALL the price our ancestors had to pay. What is important to you today. Everyone is like little children under a spell, ferries, jennies, superman, unicorns, a man from hell, what a life, living up to others' expectations. There's no magic here just truth, how could you enjoy your lifestyles. You got it, I got it, hold on to it, and never let it go. Please don't let it go. What you got is unique giving it up, the same thing you accept is going to disappoint you. You got rhythm, grace, and the mobility, with the necessary smile, keep singing, and dancing, that's the joy you bring to our hearts. You got it I got it, all they are trying to do is confuse our minds. Look good, there's much too learn, they thought us to live in fear of our self, they think they are authorities, but they are only self-ordinated. Some belief in evolution. Since the beginning of time man has looked up to the skies for something greater, higher, than himself. Theories where man came from animals, and plants. Some believe in creation, they believe in a God which created man, some believe in themselves, to them, evolution is only just a theory, and God does not exist. From within myself, I look to the east. It doesn't matter your belief system, life is no fantasy. I am perfect, beautifully, and wonderfully created, the ultimate proof, I am one of a kind. We are all one of a kind. It's not an imaginary world we are living in existence I have only one direction, reason, and purpose, I have to live, my God, by its commands. I beat the odds, the burden I have to carry is so extraordinary, I don't even know how I get it done. It's a digital world everyone is vainly forgetful, unaware of a universe that keeps on bring forth precious life, exempt from stain, immaculate, gigantic, intuitive, full of grace, and strength. I lead here, more a great king today that that of ancient times.

THE MAN OF A POET

IN THE MIND OF A POET, THERE'S VISIONS plucked right out of the thin air. Inspiring, not being idle, standing by the wayside, calmness, in meditation, the inner being could transport the spirit too reality. In the mind of a poet is a natural force of nature, seven continents, seven seas, the wonder of the stars in an expanding universe. A reader, writer, of the daily dramatics, shocking, strange, effect on mankind. Distance undiscovered civilizations. The pen as a navigator. In the mind of a poet, is to call out the disguises, reality, fact, fiction, versus the adoration becoming alternate truth of the day in a chaotic world. In the mind of a poet, children having children, innocent victims of the system, corrupted politicians, depleting fertile soil, air, and water pollution, in the atmosphere, and the control of food storms, and the control of the population.

NO NUCLEAR WEAPONS

WE NEED NO NUCLEAR WEAPONS, ERMA WILL put out your mushroom cloud. A hurricane is a devastating force of nature. As the place was quiet and calm, suddenly flashflood warning, quick as she appeared, she disappears moving, until she returns. You going to need help, lots of help, reserved energy were stored in her. Clouds. The earth was mad at us. Erma brought, rolling thunder, lightning bolts, lights bright, a greater heat, than the surface of the sun. There was no specific point of entry, from any angle she came. Beware, she's creeping up slowly, category four gusting winds, rapid speeds, over 200mph. Radars better keep on track on her, entry could come from any point, any angle. Tornadoes, landslides, major flooding in the cities. Love her, or hate her, I don't know, Erma is tremendously dangerous. We need no more nuclear weapons.

ADDICTION TO DRUGS

I LIVE A RICH HEALTHY LIFE, WORKING HARD as I never did before, aggressive, purposely, driven, with a mission to be accomplished, I always give my hundred percent, ahead of your games. Not too fast, not to slow, steady as she goes, it's a crucial moment in my life. I beat all odds, understanding the enemies. I am odd until to joy in my heart, having fun in life, all of my life, I have no fear, at all, for anything, your addiction, don't be a victim, no one can help you out but yourself, your bad habits, keeping you back in life, one way to quit is to quit, drop the old habits. You are not thinking you are a victim, there's a serious problem. Think about it, your future is at stake. Cocaine is dangerous, don't let no one introduce you to coke remember your family first, they love you the most, there's always hope. Many people are depending on you. Denying there's a problem, is so suspect, admitting it's your first step in your development, all it takes is a small amount, to take away everything, seven times to fall, seven times to rise, now it's how you respond to your circumstances, you be the judge, there is huddle to cross. I hold anyone in high esteem, I induce him who overcomes his demons of addiction. I am a drug-free man, this is no time for mediocracy it may be too late, time flies when you are having fun. You don't know what you are doing, you not thinking. Don't use cocaine, you don't need it, do not let it use you as it slaves, where is your, pride and ambition. Hosting a demon. Set my people free, let them be, free in life, bending their back like mules, carrying the weight like two-legged fools can't see you are playing with trouble, twice defeated, blind, bound by chains.

The life you choose to live is having lifelong effects on many. Those that are concern about your selfish attitude, it's a kind of toll on, taking away, adding, sorrows, and pain baggers, vagabonds, coke is for fools, anyone could make mistakes in life but don't ever offer cocaine to me, you should be thankful to be alive, everyone deserves a second chance, now you are in a good position to help others.

SMILE

THE WHOLE WORLD COULD BE SMILING, I GUESS you want to know what I am talking about, and heard it many time before, so I will say it again, danger walks with smiling faces, some you have to let pass by say him and bye, bye. Trust no one at this time. You could see a man face, you can't read his mind, you can't see his heart. So who are you, are you my brother, from a friend, this is forever true, without end. Is that too much to offer? Or too little too late? When I see you, I see myself, is that too much to ask? No one could think of everything. Telling little tales, deceiving myself, you can't forgive until you forget, remember the most important detail a fool has no discretion drawing attention that seems to be a lot of fun to him. Until one day he ran into a sudden stop. If you try to hide the truth you will eventually get caught. Play by ears, cease every opportunity to listen and learn. Remember the truth is certain, you will never win. Do not be headstrong, never interested in what others have to say. Self-opinionated, want to hear yourself, have the last word. People would say anything they want to stay, it's a simple way, it won't put them in expense, talk is cheap, sometimes very irritating, how they quickly forget, they can't see their tails, and the whole world is smiling.

BE COMFORTABLE WITH YOURSELF

THE NUMBER ONE PRIORITY IS TO BE COMFORTABLE with yourself, smile. Like a clown, if you want to, show your happy face. Smile with the world. Who cares, behind that smile is a special face, one I know I would like to kiss, you don't play, I am sure you only do it to show that you care. Wipe that frown from your face, and put a beautiful smile in its place, sick or sad, and feeling blue. You could keep on smiling too. When you smile with the world, it will smile right back at you. Let that smile light up the world, with love, and harmony.

NOTHING IS FREE

YOU WERE BORN WITH PECULIAR TALENT AND SKILLS. Potential, and gifted ideas. But here is where it all will begging to develop nothing is free. Working hard, driven by passion. With the right motivation you can do anything, anything is possible, you put your mind to. After all, we got to learn to walk before we can run. There is no one way of measuring success. There's always going to be mountains of challenges. To test your will. Doing it right the first time, it won't need fixing. Is your confidence. Some clouds hold no vapor which cease to exist without forming rain. Make your pitch, but distance stars pitches, and you wish, and wonder if your dreams would ever come true. Wake up, your future is a much, more beautiful place, stop our crying leave your sorrows, and pain, giving in to your fears. When I see you crying in know is your heart aching, hurt, who is going to stop the tears from falling, no one would trade your place. No one has been to heaven or hell, and back again to tell what they have witnessed. The problem is in our mind, life is full of incredible people, at the drop of a dime you could be next champion, and it took skill and your expertise, in all our activities to create the possibilities.

RAYS OF LIGHT

ONE OF LIFE'S MOST INSPIRATION IS SECRET LOVE. The shades were gray as night, and the nightshade of gray turn into rays of light. When you say you love someone let it be for the perfect reason, don't tell me you love me and turn around, and hurt my feeling, it may be too late to say you are sorry. I never saw it coming. It's not right to force anyone too love you, set me free, love is free, the choices of our free will. When the glass is broken it can't be fixed anymore. Keep your promises, you never know they maybe all the defense you have. There are moments in love you could never be prepared for it. Was clear to me sometimes our words are contrary to our actions. How you heal a broken heart, full of burning pain, and desire. It appears it wasn't worthy of loving you. Love has put us through a lot of difficult periods in our lives, and still, there was a progress that ends up critical too saving our relationship. There are moments when love is at its best when you love for the right reason.

LET US TALK

KEEP NOT SILENT, IF WHAT YOU HAVE TO say is meaningful, and worth listening too. Come, let us talk, I enjoy good, interesting conversations, I give you my word. Communication is an important skill for our use. Whether we communicate by words. Symbols, characters, signs, son, our language express thoughts and ideas. We don't have to be intelligent, intellectuals, choice words with meaning represent our expressions, carrying the authority of our communicative skills. The utterance acts by the power of the word in action. If we lose our communicative skills. We love everything. So come, let us talk, maintaining the practice of our communicative abilities will get the word out. The art, and skill of executing the word in all areas for any reason to accommodate in our daily task. I believe in the word as a person who will tirelessly in the moral importance of the word to the adequate usual needs of communication. I employ myself in a steady undertaking of which things are to be done. Word sound power, come, let us talk, let us communicate.

THE BEST PART OF THE DAY

CATCH THE EARLY PART OF THE MORNING, AND get the best part of the day. Life is not to complicated me all I want is to be free. Many challenges, where some have succeeded many have failed. The stress is calling in a stone-cold world. No one knows in which direction to turn where are we heading. It's better to be safe than sorry, a man of principle is a man amongst men how far is the bottom, their life is a ball, leaving me with your leave over crumbs. A man of distinction must always do what's right, just too prove you wrong. You know the truth, and hide it, I had to write this poem. A little is never enough from the top. I will live a rich healthy life, hear the poor when they cry. Rich in body, mind, and spirit, which is wise. Think twice everyone is responsible for their actions, view, and beliefs, some more unusual than strange. Resurrection, insemination, so who is the judge, where were good or bad. There must be the reason why I am at liberty to think for myself it's no mystery, the journey may seem long but life is short.

COMPLEX MIND

IT WAS IN AN IMAGINARY STATE, SUDDENLY M Y thoughts drifted away, and any attempt I made to put my state of mind into perspective, meaningful, thoughts, I was thinking, whatever happens in the transcendental moment, the complexities of my mind could not understand how to sustain. To understand it's complexities, sharing thoughts of the experience, drifting, as I could, from one pole to the next. I was existing in the spiritual realms; the possibility of explanation changes my perception of everything. If I had known the center to the edge the omnipresent manifestation would be revealed, and pacify explain. Only in my thoughts of an imaginary state, I have changed my perception.

TIME CHANGES THINGS

MY THOUGHT WAS ON YOU TODAY, I THOUGHT of you and I smile. I thought of my love for you. My thought was on your heartily smile, I love you, and I hope your love shall return, because of where we came from, and all we have been through, my entire being, of existence eternally remain in this reality. I wonder very frequently why some people act within such reserve, I assume over time thing always change yes, time changes everything. But anything is also possible by the order existing in nature. Something very special is about to happen. You are about to see a brand new me, my spirit is accelerating to the motion that summits my infinite love. It's another time and the right place. A world in which I will long remember, expressing the same reality of ourselves mostly in the audience, where the subject is on love.

VISION THE FUTURE

I WAS SITTING IN MY ROOM, AND I sense a mode of inspiration, within myself, my emotion wants to be free, at that moment, my being became still as silence, every thought became complicated, discipline did overcome one the spirit within the body, which is man's temple, perfect for a spiritual intervention, where spiritual bonds are formed, vibrating the physical part I must play, moving my thought to meditation. I ascended, it doesn't take much planet earth, just a vision of the future. Mysteries in the cycle of things. Mankind doesn't bother me, mankind is a funny creature, strange, but interesting. I can't imagine what I can't see. I am just a simple man giving thanks, and praises. But out of darkness coming light. I am light, I am darkness, I live, mankind has achieved monumental accomplishment. I shall attain to it, knowledge, and understanding. I am not worthy of wisdom too high for me. I am not a foolish man. No one knows everything, there's always a new thing to experience under the sun. Why angels are in the servitude of the highest God. Mysteries are there to open my mind. I was created in my image, after, my likeness, I hope everyone is behaving well on earth, here comes the universe I could feel the vibration, it doesn't take much to be inspired, fell the earth, air, water, and the sunshine. All of life is a cycle with the universe.

ACCEPT LIFE FOR WHAT IT IS

SAVE ME YOUR NAME STATUS, UTMOST RESPECT, AND prominence. It doesn't matter who you think you are. Let me live, live in harmony, in the symphony, which nature design, and so brilliantly display. Live free, and brave, put your whole heart into life. Accept life for what it is. There are many lives to live, the magic language, is a smile on your face. One to live, one to die, from the dawn of time. Through the ages to ancient times. Life has accomplished its mission. Old things are being renewed. Life is here, there, and everywhere, existing in the most remote, inhospitable, place. Life expands way beyond that which the eyes could see. We think we can defy all logic, understanding, imagination, and consciousness. Symbolic events which took place in the past are most likely to reoccur in the future. The universe is a broad, and wide place if we could call it a strangely unique place. The one journey we know not what to expect. Life is a constant, coexisting story between where order we can begin too tame. The sunlight's up the day time, and the moon could shine at nights, no surprises, and tomorrow would be another day. The reality is the only time, which stands the test of time.

AFRICA, IS CALLING

HOW LONG SHALL THE WICKED RULE OVER my people all that is destructive has the nature of fire. Stop those colonial power, pirates, and conquers, return all the land that was stolen from us. African, your drums are calling, the rhythms are in me, move to the beat, communicating once again. Turning the hands of time, it's better to be late than never, my home is my struggles. Struggling for a united Africa. It is important to be there. To take what belongs to us, sign, sealed, and delivered, that land is ours. Our ancestors sacrifice for us to create a greater future, it's never too late my warriors fighting for freedom, and justice, never too late my brother, and sister.

DEVIL'S PLAYGROUND

MANHATTAN, EAST SIDE, I grew up in the neighborhood, an opportunity is a cease commodity. It needs to pick up, people crying, some are dying, the place is untidy, idle youth on the corner, the devil playground. I was trying to run a small business in the community. What is standard, what is covered up. Whether you save a little or you save a lot. Anyone with the potential deserves the chance to grow. Black or white, rich or poor, how you look, and where you live. It's too arbitrary and ambitious to the fact of being financially independent. Trust in the process which bonds each party's interest. Application accepted and approved of your bank loan. It will pick us up from the floor, in the bank.

I LOVE WOMAN

SOME OF MY MOST IMPORTANT INSPIRATIONAL SECRET OF love has been revealed, I love woman, one of the stronger forces of nature is her love. She's my queen, my companionship, my familiar friend, and mate. Her responsibility I don't have a clue about it as yet. Power came from her womb, eve of man, beautiful creations. My word is my bond, my principles are my promise to always keep. For your love, I will single-handedly play my role. Like a piece of cake, a walk in the park. Woman, I know you are all that I need. You are my imaginary army, one -man band, you are my back up chorus. Tener, and bass, triple bar, immensely instrumental to my life, you bring sweet music too my hear, her love is truly amazing the responsibility now rests on the woman to bear the pain since the beginning of time. Now that you know where you came from, be thankful, give praises to the woman. One of the stronger forces of nature is her love. The woman is a master.

TOP OF THE MORNING

IT'S NEVER TOO LATE, YOU HAVE A CHOICE to do what is right, and necessary. I say, top of the morning, it's the dawn of a brand-new day. I say I have accomplished so many things before the sunrise, while you were still trying your best to get some sleep. For a guilty conscience, there are never any soft pillows. They are not going to get a good sleep no time, not tonight, all their try to pretend their life is in grand good shape. The life they are living is like they are living in hell, it's so easy, without thinking, they would take your life away. Don't try to impress them, big fish always eat the small shrimps. Watch it, all on their mind is vanity. It's their continuous distraction, material, interest is to gain, it's a means to an end. Wealth, power is their desperation, to gain your sympathy, they would cheat, do anything to gains. A guilt conscience, there is never a soft pillow, top of the morning it's the dawn of a brand new day.

IF THIS WORLD WERE MINES

YOU ARE THE ARCHITECT OF YOUR WORLD, YOU know the blueprint of your golds, let us get this wheel in motion. We have made insufficient progress. We have to create our environment in consciousness with each other, but I hope you find what you are searching for, if this world were mined everyone would be having fun, unfortunately, it's not. But in giving we shall receive eyes have never seen anything like this, we are inspired to think for ourselves, in everything, actively, negatively, and positively. It is a culture of aggression, acting like you are the purest thing, innocent and we are a guilty of some heinous crime. A tribute to your self-worthiness. I have never experienced anything like this in my life but this is the dawn of a brand-new age for mankind. Making a living is all a man may ever need. This is institutive, that is understood the reality is we are a strange people to you, with big ideas, we have no time to complain. Times change, so we should move with the time. Never put yourself in a position of dependency, people would do so much for you, be independent in your thinking in a time where no one is willing to assist you in your aim, and objectives. We have a mind of our own, we know how to operate our own. We know how to organize ourselves, a lot of love, and unity, no fears. We are the visionary of this time. It is going to take communication.

HOMELESSNESS

DIRTY, AND DANGEROUS. I HEAR THEM SAYING, LOOK at them, like garbage on the street corners. They are always on the streets begging for money or something to eat. Look at them they are so untidy but all they need is for you to be compassionate, show some love. With all the amazing life you are enjoying today, this could sure happen to anyone. Homeless, nowhere to live, on the streets whole day, every day. Homeless, and alone like a sinking ship, no rescue, no help is on the way, lost in darkness, nowhere to go, going around in circles, most people don't know, don't even care about your situation, the hardship that you have to face. No one believes in you anymore as you don't have any faith in yourself in your world. Loser they call him. All you need is someone to show some love in their soul. Be a compassionate human and be compassionately caring all the time. I need a beautiful spirit to occupy this space I don't know where, and what happened when it went wrong since there was nowhere to turn, it had been downhill on. My soul is sorrowful and restless, all I could do is pray for someone to watch over me, put my mind at ease, let me get a little rest. Nothing I could say or do will justify this position. All I could do now is discuss what I have learned.

RASTAFARI

HOW EXCELLENT IS THY NAME, YOUR GLORY IS above heavens. Out of the mouth of babes, and suckling's thou has obtained strength. It's a natural mystic, he's the mighty one, high is this man. The emotion of my heart, I see it in his eyes. He is upon his girl, sitting on his throne, he is a nobleman, honorable leader field marshal general. His foundation is in the holy mountains of Zion, he that dwelt in the secret place of the highest, shall abide under the shadow of the almighty. The Lord Loveth the gates of Zion more than all the dwelling places of Jacob. Haile Selassie I Rastafari. King of kings, Lord of Lords, conquering lion of the tribe of Judah. The government shall be on his shoulder and a little child shall lead the way. Fighting the aggressor, clear up the transgression, set his people free. Rastafari, Kada Mawi, Kada Mawi.

TRIBE

MUSIC, SOUND, MY ENVIRONMENT, NOT EVEN CONCRETE COULD stop the beat I don't like promises, promises are a comfort to a fool, without money, life is really funny, give me something I can crave, and it's beautiful to my ears. Not when you want to, music is a gift, give me music. Life is much like a music sheet, music alone shall live forever, music is my choice. A gift to mankind, it's not often you see a man having fun. It's like magic, I have never felt anything better in my life than music. Play music, it's the best vibes a man can get. It's a part of our heritage and culture, where does it come from, all over the atmosphere, here, there, and everywhere. Where does it go, everyone, everything love the sound, music is a universal language a spiritual experience, the beauty of nature, wonder of the universe, at work, I highly recommend it, I love music, keep it burning in my soul, a perfect firestorm to soothe my shaking nerves. You can dance, you can sing, you can sing, and dance, you can swing, you can rock to it, you can do anything you can imagine. Rise the sleeping dead, and making him move to it. Play music, play music, play music, can't even help yourself, dance fast or slow, reap what you sow, it's out of this world, it's magic, it's nature's law. It flows all around, what goes up must come down. Hit it, let the blessing flow, keep it on the air, working hard each day. It's my winning lotto, whenever music play in the atmosphere, experience life in all to glory.

STORY OF ETHIOPIA

THE SUN SHALL NOT SMITE ME BY DAY, or the moon by night, the lord is my Sheppard, I fear no evil. I look to the hills from where come thy help, my help comes from Jah! Whom they hate, and have not to love. If you were to write the story of your life, what would it be? Where would you start? I, would not keep silent, I would start from within my heart. I could not keep silent to a heavy conscience, for the lack of a positive response. Not to offend anyone, being careful, never to put material gain to generosity give me life, happy or sad, past, present, future, and beyond, satisfy my soul, higher than, I am, I am living man, every day. If it is something good, and useful, you better share it, prince, and princess shall come out of Egypt, Ethiopia shall soon stretch forth her hands unto God. He shall be a wonderful councilor, the mighty God. The eternal father, the prince of peace. When all was readers a spoiled mule was brought to carry him, Ras Makorinem, the few yards from where he had been waiting to the front of the door of the house he entered behold the luminescent baby, and offering a pray, that unlike all of his previous of fearing by Yas Himabet, that the son might survive his infancy.

A LIGHT SHINING AROUND ME

I AM IN A LION'S DEN, AND AN army is up against me. My heart is pumping blood in my chest, chest-beating, life breathing, living man. Let them left fuss, and fight. I live in love; love is all I have to give. Can't see you see there is a light shining all around me. The journey I am on is not my own, the journey I am on is one of love, I hope to inspire others along the way. I looked into myself, left, and right, I could feel the vibes, they pass me by. Hi, show teeth, fake smile, living in their world. They have no love, o it sucks a pity, not fully aware of the darkness in their life. They need to look into themselves, it's a mystic vibration. Sharing love, no doubt about it.

SATISFY YOUR EMOTION

MY BASIC INSTINCT EVOLVES AND MERGED LIKe I knew this was meant to be, I knew from the start, sometime someplace before. I don't play any games, the stars up above were designed, for perfect love, and harmony I knew somehow you existed, it's just the beginning I will satisfy your emotion in all seasons. I will treat you as my queen, enough to be your king. I commit, passionately, internally, in love with you, everyone must make their own choice, but I owe you the compliment. Girl my massage is authentic, legit, come on, let us make a plan, my purpose here is in full time on the job, girl, all I need is your love, I cannot wait any longer, I hope you don't need anything else above my love. I need your love, right here with me is where you belong. I need your love at the crack of dawn, you were born to be love, let me satisfy your emotion tell the morning comes, I love you before you ever dream to exist.

SACRIFICE

IT IS A CHALLENGE, MONEY MELTS DOWN. YOU got to make some sacrifice in life or you could lose everything, it looks like you are not getting any sleep, make sure you weigh out every option. You have a beautiful home, and family you want to keep it, right. You spend more than you earn, you got to know the reality. Taking care of yourself is another luxury, not your needs. You work hard everyday, you are a moron and when it comes to your money, buying all sorts of things you do not need, you are going to need a lot of money. Having all types of discussion but not about finances. That says who you are, now you got to forget your wants, and they take care of your needs, credit cards, high-end cars, vacations, toys. You got to know where the money going to come from, you got to take care of your finances; wake up to your money reality. There are things so obvious to you, but you are not thinking, you better keep an eye on your money. Family, you got to know your priorities, your financial future is at risk. You got to feel the pressure, it's going to feel exhausted, headache, and pain. When it comes to shopping you are the pro, your life capital has gone down to zero, thousands of dollars in debts, you have the last act, paying thousands of dollars in interest in five years or less, even in the next few weeks everything gone.

SPIRITUALLY CONNECTED TOO NATURE

YOU COST ME A WHOLE LOT, YOU HAVE no clue what you have done for me. What I when through it's time to reclaim our history. Silence makes a mighty noise, as words are put into action. What has been hidden from the wise, and prudent has revealed to babe and sucklings. The sunrise for all, the other half that has never been told. Black was here first, spiritually connected to nature, and the universe. If you believe you shall be deceived, the truth is within yourself. Leave me under neat a canopy of stars, enough of your old times' point of view of things, our eyes are open to those who are responsible for the depreciation of the plane, every heritage, and culture, reclaim the earth, take care of where we all live. The reaction is no fairy tale. You are draining the earth of her natural resources. Operating on material gain. The truth is an offense but not a shame.

LET THEM TALK

THEY KEEP TALKING, LET THEM TALK. IT'S EITHER they are too early or too late. I don't care what the critics have to say, I know they think they are better because they are more fortunate. I am special, you are special that's the way it is supposed to be, that's the way to feel, don't judge me, don't call me names. I have to struggle, you don't know me, and you've done the same. I don't do normal things I am highly motivated, to accept less than my worth is unacceptable, you got to read through the line, think for yourself, it's too simple for a curious mind. Leave the symmetric is too corrosive to the truth. Have a vision of reality, aiming high, in your golds, and objectives, am not any way your criticism could possible help me, I am on the wonder list, anything I touch turns into a pot of gold.

THIS LIFE IS NOT SCRIPTED BET

SOMETIMES I WONDER ONE DAY IF WE ALL shall be free. Who am I, where did I come from, how did I get here, still there are no answers. The worse of nature, bring out the best nature in mankind. A storm is brewing, life is a secret well kept I will be shaping waterfalls, carving landscapes to remain a fountain is not too accomplish away of my golds. I am going to tell it my way. If you place a fish in a fish bold and teach it to be a bird, it still will not drown, adapt, or die, that is how it is done here, never back down. Fire, water earth, wind, forces of nature transforming the geographic structure of the land, improvise, every day our lives are being shaped. You have more in common with the stars, that anything existing right here on earth, you are one unique individual, there is none, no life like yours, parallel to in this entire universe. Life is a lesson well in this entire universe. Life is a lesson we learn over some time in our own experiences. About you, about people, everyone connected to the sun, moon, and stars. Life is a gift entirely yours, how could you leave a universe which is connected to everything, shaping our lives daily.

IT'S A NATURAL BEAUTY

CULTURE IS LOVE, ITS' OUR WORLD, CULTURE IN my heart, I will speak my mind, it's time, dance if you want to, dance, sing if you want to, sing. Culture is good for you, so we share it. Lots of togetherness is the spirit within us want to be free, the love we feel for the people. Celebration the unification inspiring our country. Culture is colorful brilliance it's music, food, that's the way we feel, can't stop m we don't embrace religion, we embrace our heritage. I will put it above the world, let the truth be manifest itself, let us see us see who would be justified. Whose culture is the best? You got yours, and I got mines. Our ancestors gave us. Culture is love. Defy the dog to moan the minds of the people. I will forgive, but I will never forget. You were neither satisfied, your love only brought me pain, no smile, only chains. We don't want to assimilate into another man culture, why? We already have our own culture, to share with this life, culture loves your way, your lifestyle. Not your culture of vanity, and fear. But culture is our revolutionary unrest.

NO VISION

WITH ALL THE INFORMATION AND KNOWLEDGE WE HAVE, we have achieved nothing. The fact is still floating around. The thing has never changed. The world leaders still lack the vision for the future. In the twenty-first century still looking for the prospect to world peace. They don't know what life is worth, they know the truth, and hide it. They don't know what we know, forget all the truth they are talking about. From the dawn of time, they begin, try, and failed. The target is on the black child, keep it real, let's end this right now, there's hardly a good day in my world. My life, there must be more reason to life than just to live and die. End the game, black people were first on creation, we have no one to blame, we are wise as anyone that ever exist. Since the dawn of time, you chose the wrong foe, it's good over evil I am black and beautiful, you have that, now is big trouble, separate the good from the bad. Measure life by what you make of it. Think you need it because you running out of time. The world is cold. Many in their suffocation. The consequences of your actions. Listen carefully, and learn, repeating the same mistake over, and over again, you don't make it easy, you are the worse enemy. No self-respect, stick around you could learn a lot. Two wrong can't make it right, listen to your heart, don't stab me in the back. Hate is an image, your ways pass that, is a battlefield. You want us to take each other's lives, kill or be killed. Like you have done many times before. I could name a few. Who's next on their list. Could be you could be me. It either to stick around or run like hell, bullets start flying lay flat it not the cross, it's a gun. The target is the black man, the future world leader.

DIANA

DIANA WAS A BEAUTIFUL PRINCESS, WHO WAS a victim of her circumstances, rejected by the royal family. Call to play the role she undertook with purpose and sense of duty. Diana was a strong, confident woman of action, a trendsetter, soft-spoken, never silent, her voice awaked the world. There would never be someone like Princess Diana, our princess she shall ever remain. it's clear, her love for the poor, and helpless. Marginalize, and the ridicule, radiate in the universe in the weary hearts she touched, but a destructor to the system status quo. Princess Diana lives forever in my heart, one of the most important women in history., there would never be the next Diana, her radiance lit up the universe, the works she performs were sacred.

ALL THINGS IS TOO KNOW ABOUT LOVE

IT WOULD TAKE A LIFETIME TO UNDERSTAND ALL there is to know about love. The first step I self-love, nothing is wrong with that. But forgiveness is choosing to love, spiritually it could poppel you to the stars. When the heart gives over to what it has lost, the spirit rejoices over what it has left, there's much to know. We could never understand, the two of us with one burning desire, love is what kept us together. Love will always remain in our heart, that nothing could ever destroy. Love has done us well, but holding on to a love that do you wrong, chances, changes were swift, and remarkable, while it seems you were making all the right moves, love, the heart is a symbol of love. Love is the foundation pillars building block, the duration of happiness is to love and be love.

BLACK WOMAN, THE FIRST

HUDDLES OBSTACLES, STUMBLING BLOCKS, NOTHING COULD STOP YOU. If they would try and fine a woman like you, they would try. Black woman, you are my story. You have my word, this is my commitment to you from the dawn, in the beginning, black woman, you are the first extraordinary one, the ultimate woman. The bliss, and beauty of civilization. Your foundation could never be remove from history. The responsibility to carry the black child. Black woman you bear man, male, and female, you did bear man, God created man, male, and female, he did created man. I have given it every thought, pondering, giving up all others, in this world. Loving you is to make my fantasies into a reality. I will always come through for you, it's true. I am not living in an imaginary world. When you love, somethings are there as perfect proof. Black woman you bring sunshine into my world, and light up my life I love you like stars up above in the night sky. More than money, silver, diamond, rubies, and gold black woman, I love you for who you are, has anyone seen her, not for the way you look. Black woman, you are the only one for me, nothing to stop me now, please, hurry up, and come home to me. I am lonely, don't let me wait on you too long. I am crazy, and sad, don't leave me crying shedding tears, my aching heart, letting my emotion is getting to me, your love has gotten me ill. Return to me, when you are away this house is not a home, woman we complement each other. You are my universe without you what kind of world, my world will turn out to be?

ZION

SOME PEOPLE WANT TO GO TO ZION, ON believers on their wild imaginations, on make dreams, to reveal the thing that are right, one must express themselves it's a complicated issue get the stifling truth from off your chest, I see Zion every day, I see Zion in the rising sun, I see Zion in the morning, children take a walk with me, let us discover the promise land, here we would have lots of fun. Zion is in my head, its's a spiritual vibes, let us a have a good time, Zion is the promise land, I see Zion as my home, too much oppression is on this land, too much confusion, corruption is polluting the atmosphere, what to be shall be, there got to be a revolution, the whole world is crying out for change poor people is crying out for help, children in the ghettoes are suffering. Where there is a will there is a way. Where is the happiness. Our ancestors deserved more than what you had to offer, today's children want more than just a dream, it's a brand-new day. The road is rocky, and rough, and it ain't getting any better, when are they going to be alright. What more could you do to the door, children we got to liberate ourselves. From bondage soling slaver has took it's told, on our body, mind and spirit. This is a new age, we have to trod mount Zion way. To be free is a must Zion is a place of new beginnings.

WOMAN WALK WITH ME

WOMAN, WALK WITH ME, AS THE SUN CONTINUES to shine, the moon, and stars endures the darkness of the nights. Woman walk with me. Each day my heart keeps pumping blood through my veins. Doing what is good, and acceptable making me worthy of my purpose, and my being. Woman walk with me, let me erase that frown from off your face, and put a hearty smile. In its place. Your love I will continue to reserve. Never have I found a better love than yours in my life before. Woman walk with me, you provide all I need, the things you offer are multiple good. I quit searching, why should I continue to search? I keep reminding myself when I have found a love like no other before. Woman walk with me, the joy, and happiness your love has brought to my life, preserved a place with your virtue, and grace, don't you ever quit, walk with me on this journey, every step I make, every step of the way, walk with me by your beauty flowing through your veins. Woman walk with me your sacrifice will make us one indeed.

KNOCK, KNOCK

GET RID OF THE DISEASES BEFORE IT REPLICATES, isolate them like a dangerous virus before they react and spread. Your mentality need to change a strange but powerful thing. Knock, knock, did get your attention yet. They think they know it all, they think they know everything. They think they are the gift of the world. What is their source of thinking, everything they try it failed. They want to gain everything in this world, knock, knock, did I get your attention yet, loser never win. At an all-time low, no self-respect, and ambition. It is quite possible a lot of people are going to get push around by your wild egos. Not one step further, stop your isolating around. Your aims, and objective, boasting, and exulting yourself. Knock, knock, did I get your attention yet, let things unfold naturally for themselves. You are now beyond repair, you have no intention to place fare, remember principle maketh man, we all have to grow up eventually. Thing are living up on their own naturally, life goes on anyhow. What has happened in the past it's quite possible it could recur all again. A strange panorama, superstitious, myth, some people call it facts. Knock, knock, did I get your attention yet, one day is all it would take to know.

IT IS NOT A MOVIE

THIS IS NOT A MOVIE, EVERYTHING WE EXPERIENCE here is real. There's a lot of destruction terrified people, it's a dangerous time in the neighborhood, my family can even go outside it's not safe to wake the streets anytime. If you want to go you must say, if you want to go, it your way, do, die, or runaway, they would eat the food off your plate one crook get away in a vain, the other two get up and run, one teen was only seventeen, he may not live to see another birthday. One survive to stand trial, crime, gun violence. Little kid, going outside use to be a big thing, now, it's just another risk, robbers, and cocaine invading our sanctuary, parent are concern about what is happening in the community. There are in need of some discretion, and comforting advice, worried about thing getting worse. This thing would break them down, thing is coming more difficult each day. They know thing, see things, feel things they never felt before. I give up on everything, it just another bad day. Now new information. The situation has become completely on the abnormal scale. I thought I was done crying, I am still crying, I lost my purpose I give up on everything. Until my sense of purpose has been restored, life in the city I don't get it, I just don't get it.

DEJAVU

WHAT IS THIS SENSATIONAL FEELING, I AM FEELING, mystically, I was here before, like I am here again? What on earth could be happening here now. My spirit is going through a strange moment. A most shocking experience outside myself, out of my body, this prism was not clear to me. I wanted to be right where I am, I didn't want to stay, but I don't want this experience to end, I may never experience it again. I was caught, red handed day dreaming in the fears of the unknown. I was trying to figure out, can this be real, or coincidence. The reality of my experience, two of the same kind insanity, intensively. Then I begin to understand the vibes, instinct is a need to our survival skills it's just what I would have voted on, but I had to listen wisely to the voice. The human fabric is burning out in the cities. Experience more here consciously, but subconsciously, somewhere else. Dejavu, something is going on, strange, but no to unusual to me. Consciously you can do all four corners of the earth, consciously you can be more that on wave length loving our own unique experience float around the world, and back again, from one place to another, places inside of tomorrow. The emotional mechanics that operate, the common, and the abnormal there is shade of gray between these places there's always pride in the mission.

LET US TALK

I HAVE BEEN SPENDING TIME DAILY, TRYING TO communicate with you. Would you like to talk with me, I think we have a lot in common that we can share, youth, does not deny strength, and intelligence, and where there is age there is reason, an open mind view things from many different angles, open a box of constructive topics, in, out, up, down, side by side, in every dimension. Let us talk of understanding, truth, and love. Let us take a good look at the main issue, and present new and useful ideas. With substance, insight, with pin point, accuracy. Let us talk with integrity on any level of understanding, confident in what we say, saying only what we mean. let us use the power of the word in a positive sense of influence not against ourselves, and other, caring ourselves with honor, and dignity, at the bacon, beam, there I want to be. The universe, we came, and meet it as it is through the ages with all it's awesome, wonders, and mysteries. The sun, moon, and stars, the birds, and the trees, the sea, and the skies. This whole, world belongs to you, and I, we could never create, don't ever try, and take anything away. They are the reason why we are still alive here them as they are. We only just getting started, we only just begin, be someone with purpose, as a witness, do something for once in your life to contribute to this creation. It is so critical, they are the one, our teachers, it's life is cosmic.

SPIRITUAL WAR

LISTEN PEOPLE IT'S NOT AS BAD AS YOU may think, who know better must do better, we are the force behind everything, we could make our dreams turn into reality, just listen to the voice of nature. They are after my head, and I know they are after you, and I, the road is slippery and wet, beware of the many tricks, and traps hit hard, watch the pit falls. Wounded, I see them badly hurt, they did not die, but they are ready for a fall, this is a serious time, they are terrorizing the people, it is so outrageous. They are trying to run away. I see them going up in flames, isn't this rebellious time. Their sins have multiplied to the heavens completely burning down to ashes. It's a spiritual war, spiritual weakens in highland, and low places, fighting, flesh, and blood, we can't leave them with minor injuries. Long time we have been trying we have to act fast we can't give up, how many time we have bashed our heads against the wall. Now we see the light, even with my eyes close, I could still see them clear. I feel they are near, and I have no fear, don't matter what they say, or what try to do. My heart is pure, I am righteous man, I am not asleep, gone clear. Here I am then.

MY WORLD IS COLORFUL

I AM PERFECT, BEAUTIFULLY CREATED. I EXIST FROM on the inside out. My world is colorful, super powerful, fire, life over death. Reproducing, procreating, circulating, determine to manifest itself. I must celebrate life, steading out itself. No one knows when it started, but it is my privilege, and honor just being here. Art bringing to life a sculptured, detail. I am that entity, man, lion in me, elements, living organism. I am from particular order, with the essential tool to serve mankind. Like the universe colliding particles exploding. It's a colorful world, one which took years in the making, with countless stars all around me. Let me tell you, morning, noon, and night. I am the singular, and plural, of lights, time, and space. Physical, and spiritual being. To the rescue, the master in me has awaken. Confinement in the future, confident of myself it will depend on much moral success, something I live by fate, doing things the orderly way has become my life style.

LIFE

PLEASE RING THE BELL, SOUND THE ALARM, TIME is running out, I am trying to persuade you, life could be so unpredictable, it's not how hard we fall, it's how quick we rise up again. We could learn a lot of things about life, come let us reason about life, this could be your last chance before it is too late. A man got to make up his own mind. One thing is different from the other. Questions, and answers. What do we do with questions, and answers? What do we do with question beside asking? How do we find the answers to the questions we ask? Things are so unusual; I am ready to take the risk. One- word change everything, you cannot stop it, teach the world about life, make some cheers, life is all we need. One thing, the experience we gain cannot be match, reflecting on the questions, and answers of life, I got love, pain, joy, empathy. I am doing, alright, I am strong some people have a lot, plenty, of everything some people have a little, of nothing at all. Life teaches, but the mystery is unknown to us when you give you receive, all in life is here. To stay, do you angry with me, or are you angry, and have different ideas. You could gain all the material in the world, have you looked in the mirror lately. When it comes to life they are less confident. They trust in their wealth, making money by millions, fortunate to have a lot, they say there is a time for everything, sorry I need life what has last since time began. This could be your last chance, you can, I can to, make that move as one let us face the facts, nobody wants to die, life changes everything, there is nothing more precious than life, don't take my word for it, there is always a new beginning, you are going to get the full experience yourself, where there's life, there is hope. Who knew, now you do. Move super nova, time to move as one.

ILLUSION TOO ME

GONE IS TOMORROW, NOW THAT TODAY IS HERE again. And as today passes by, quickly replace, by yesterday. Forward into today all over again. Tomorrow, yesterday, and today. Now they are all an illusion to me. There must be a key to these mysteries. Tell me why, children can't get a proper education, why is there so many mental problems? Why our black children are dying? Police are killing them. The system is locking them up in their jails. Father disappear, go to jail, abuse for women for no reason. Time is slipping away still have a long way to go. Memories we live through every day. The days are getting dark the sun don't rise, and shine. Tomorrow, today, and yesterday, how could they be replacing. Tell me what is the key, to all it's a mystery.

BRAIN WASH EDUCATION

THERE'S A LAND FAR, FAR, AWAY, WHERE THERE'S no night only day. No darkness only light, all I need is love to take me there through my darkest hour. I will build my house on solid ground, never, ever on sinking sand. No rain can't wash it down, emaciate my mind from brain wash education, my train has entered the station, let River Jordan roll. I am going on a one-way ticket; I am going to the promise land. This train is bound to glory, I am going to a place I could call my home, put the capture into captive, and set the captive free, this train don't carry no unholy, only those who know how to sing the freedom song.

WORK IS FUN, AIN'T IT?

MORE FOR LESS, THINK ABOUT IT, DOING a service much greater than yourself. Play, play, play, work is fun, ain't it, it's not a question it's a fact of principle. Every day is work. It may seem impossible, but I got to do it any way. Work come naturally easy. It is a joy doing something what you like doing. It's very simple, all you got to do is just try it. Who stole the Monalisa, is the mafia candidate. Constantly asking questions, it's not the end, it's only one day at a time no one should do which you should have done for yourself, according to your works you shall get paid, you have to do it, what you are doing? What are you hiding? Who, are you hiding, from? Why are you holding down yourself? Come out in the open with it, success requires much hard work, no way of getting around it. If it's a good thing it could be number today. La, la, la, la, all you got to do is just try it. Motivation, perseverance, success is not to easily attained, work hard develop your skills time wasted could never be regained. Opportunities may only come in a life time work intelligently, anything is possible, all you got to do is just try. Work is fun, think about it. It is frustrating when a man cannot get no work.

FEAR

FEAR, ONE OF OUR MOST DEADLY HUMAN EMOTION. A perception of danger, real or imagine. Hearts playing tricks on our perception, a fragment of our imagination. We live in fear of what we don't understand, fear of what we cannot see, summons up by our own superstitious minds. Dear could be mistaken of lack of courage, also a weakness of the fear of failure. Living in fear would be a matter of life, and death. Fear of your own conceive could be rob you of your youth, and have you old, and gray. No one could rise in fear, it would keep you down, so rise above your fears, if not fear itself. So what is your biggest fear? Truth, lies, yourself, enemies, failing, friends, poor, living, death, losing? Fearing demons of your bad dreams?

NATURE KNOWS BEST

YEARS IF EVOLUTION, NATURE KNOWS BEST. NATURE HAS planned it to her own perfection. One day I was granted life. One day, one life, of the appointed time, I don't know why, but I can't leave I have to stay. Searching from sunrise, where is the light, day into night, night into day. Life is to celebrate, it's a good thing. It's amazing perfection, beauty is certain in the manifestation of life wake up the morning, breath the fresh air of mother nature, when I think of it, it is a good thing when you could rise up in the morning. The sun is over the mountain. Feel the light of the sun and everything is going to change. The truth needs no interpretations; the truth is self-evidence. I have to live, life is a beautiful gift. It circulates, anytime, era, age, or place. My soul exist, east is east, west being west, north is north, and south is still south, tomorrow is just a day away. Sun, moon, and stars, thousands of years to live, my most valuable possession, life not because you don't have everything material, that is not everything, money, jewelry, house, cars, keep all your riches, they cannot help me. You could die at any time walking the streets. Cancers, diabetes. Naked I enter, naked I shall leave. Give me nature, I love the sunshine. I will pursuit, wisdom, knowledge, and understanding, all through my life, it is my heart desire, I have to live, one day, one life, at the appointed time.

GOD

GOD! SO WHERE DOES THAT LEAVES US, LET'S discuss over thing to date, let's see about this cycle of complaints. Repelling, pushing, and pulling, crazy dogs, biting at each other, at the event horizon, resistance, I could hardly describe. Our mission we share is one of passion and perfect harmony. Despite the challenges we face. There's a little voice deep down inside us, the first voice, tames the most vicious beast. Brings out the best in us. Making the best of a bad situation, a smile is an authentic contract. Open to life, finally connecting, listen to that little voice.

THANKS, AND PRAISES

THANK, AND PRAISES TO THE HIGHEST, JAH ALPHA and omega. I also give thanks, and praises for, earth, wind, fire m and water. Sacredly I live as a lift up my head through your holy sanctuary. Here me when I call on your name, showing forth your praise, your light keep shinning around me, infinite, divinity. Your glory is above the heavens, as also in my life. Blessing, and anointing upon me. Guide, and protect me through, Jah! When those who will try to use all form of things to harm my being. Bless all those, keep them, care for them, adding, joy, and prosperity to their lives.

REMEMBER AFRICA

IT'S IMPERATIVE TO SHOW ARICA HOW MUCH you are proud of her. As it's important to remember Africa. We are the new builders; we are the creators. It's our duty, we have the ability don't matter how difficult. It maybe, it's time to create some change. They tried so hard with a little success to hide these facts. Africa is the land of mother of the earth, the black woman, land fertile, and green. How they could stand these facts wipe them clean from our memories, but marvel not, over these things. It's their own hunting memories which will still remain in history. Elevate the son, and daughters of the highest that rule supreme, infinite, divinity, universal rights, redefying the enemies, triumphantly. What glorious day when we reach the African shores, African land, our live is going to elevate to high heights, on that day. So wake up to the bright morning beautiful African sun rising over our head, and at nights a calm full moon above in the night sky among the twinkling stars.

IN THE SHADE

THERE'S MORE BAD MEN THAN GOOD MEN, REAL criminal get away Scott free. Living in the shade, protected by their money. While we do the time, behind bar, we don't even have any existence no assistants, heaven know this is hell. They don't give a damn all they do is lock us inn jails. Right is right, wrong is wrong, I make no excuses, but their wicked inventions is too lock us up by the thousands, their traps are set, all we round do is pray for a not guilty verdict, or a grant of clemency the president.

AGE OLD SYSTEM

THIS SYSTEM IS A VERY OLD SYSTEM, BLOOD drinking system, this system is design to lock us inn, jail. You are in title to three meals a day, a bed, you can't sleep up by six. Can't go anywhere, at times escorted, just not free. Incarcerated, think jail is nice, have you ever see on the inside of a cell, it's a box. The soul intent is to lock us inn, life is not fare, it's no fantasy, man injustice towards man. Can't do as you please, they would break your spirit the system is a fraud, mass incarceration, systematic slavery. Thousand lock up by the week, prison, here we go again. The story never ended. Only a half has ever been told, no justice, no peace, just let us be free. Oppression of the weak, what to be shall be, rejected by society. This is the reality we have to cope with, face to face, each day.

VOICES

LONG TIME WE HAVE BEEN TRAVELING THIS EARTH along life journey. Man has attained knowledge by learning, and still there are many unanswered question. The power of the word has influence many in a negative sense. Be quick to listen, slow to speak, having a positive effect. There are voices I heard. Who has inspired us, voices with individual desires, voices with self- opinions, verses what should be taught. Voices that shouldn't be heard, compromising the truth. Any person having a natural capacity of intelligence. In character, that person is a genius immune from infectious foolishness, educated from ignorance and bad attitudes. So be careful of the words you speak by first examining yourself. Not in similarities or differences but rather by reflecting on you, your own self.

WORLD IN MUCH TROUBLE, WHY?

TODAY I LIVE IN A WORLD IN MUCH trouble, I acknowledge, though some may choose to disagree not even assuming the same, denying legitimate facts. Intrigue too alternate truth, accepting lies. To us the universe is still unknown, a lot yet to be discovered. A universe slowing expanding, while the earth is scientifically shrinking, failing all-natural life on a daily basis, a mystery to our minute means to indulge, in answering, over whelming unanswered questions. With the deadly consequences pertaining to our own dumb actions. The surface reality is completely different to the surface under neat. It's quite clear we have our own uniqueness and experiences, but we are the same in many ways the past shall bear fruits for the future. The choice lies in the belief in alternate facts, versus the truth, where there's anger there's pain. Angel are in the servitude of God. If you find yourself in the dark, sit it out until your eyes can see clear in the dark again.

WHY IS IT SO?

IT DOESN'T MAKE ANY SENSE, I CAN'T UNDERSTAND, it's not what I expected, it's not all it what is turn out to be. No change, as it were yesterday, so is today, and tomorrow who knows the intent. Everything happens the way they were meant to be. The future looks unpredictable in this time all we could ever hope for is a better way. In these shocking facts, the world is a complex place, too understand it's complexities is not as simple as you may think, on an ordinary day, tell me why is it so? It's unbelievable where we could be contributing factors to society, and in other way we go through thing that we shouldn't built these things help us to understand ourselves in the reshaping of our environment, and discover what we need to change. Action speaks louder than words because if all men were created equal, if each race were human, there would only be one. Do unto other as you would have them do to yourselves, tell me why is it so?

TRANSFORM AND CHANGE

You could turn a bad situation to something positive, anything can happen, life is full of surprises. The invisible turns visible, trash into treasure. Particles made up the stars. A caterpillar was not born a butterfly. A dream is just a dream until it's turn into reality. Most things are far from finish, return back to its early stage. A lot has transform, and change but ignorance and a nasty attitude there's no excuse. But shall surely leads us into destruction.

A wise man is patient, bold, fearless as a lion, never in a haste. A whip for the horse, a bridle for the ass, a rod for the fools back. Two is better than one. Iron sharpened iron. The continence of one brightest another. A lot has transform and change but ignorance and a nasty attitude, there's no excuse, but shall surely lead us into destruction.

WINNERS

FIRST PLACE, NUMBER ONE, EVERYONE WANTS TO BE winners, and it seems like that is all on everyone mind it's a world where that's all which really matters most. Eager to impress, must prove a point, the best, the greatest, better than the rest. Save that crap, close that gap, let's end that strive. Celebrating each other individual achievements, instead of separating us, categorizing, us is where the problems start. Competition there could only be one spot, the others don't count, but first place number one, only one spot.

NATURE'S SPARK

NOW AND THEN NATURE'S SPARK DELIVERS CERTAIN SPECIFIC gifts to all of us, playing her little tricks, maybe, on more people now than ever before than we may think. Especially today it could be anyone with the potential to cultivate, and develop the natural knowledge to do better than the average individual, anyone with the necessary body, tools, ingenuity, creativity, but they are too scared of discovering an unknown positive impact. It would be a brand-new world, where sometimes the things you have been searching for has been with you your whole life. If you got it, you got it, if you don't, you don't. you are born with it, that spark is from birth. It goes everywhere you go. It lives on with you throughout your life time. We all have our own special gift of our own to possess, a dog doesn't know the use of its tail, so it continues to try any bite it off.

YOUR BEST IS GOING TO CHANGE FROM TIME TO TIME

AS I OPEN MY EYES, I SAW THE bright blue sky. It's a beautiful morning a cool breeze screaming through the wooden silks. The weather is sweet. It's a mystic coming through my window panes. I plan to live, no sorrows, no pain, what is it that make you think you are any different to me. Don's judge what the eyes don't see won't hurt if we only understand don't grieve. The only difference is our best is going to change from time to time, when you are healthy as oppose to sick. Under any circumstance, I will simple do my best, immune from the negative opinions, and actions of others. Hi, or low, love is the event, if you can feel, if you can't, too bad, bad news. You got no soul, no heart, or must be dead on the dark side. All I see is love, it's what I live for in this gift of life.

EXIST ON THE INSIDE

CALENDAR AGE, ORGANIC AGE, BIOLOGIC AGE, MAN'S AGE is not measured by numbers, I feel strongly about this. Man is a living organism, age, I figure is just a picking, filling of space in a matter of stage, man in his physical form. A cellular molecule, subatomic particle, no one has the power over this part of life. Naturally I am perfectly beautiful on the inside, I exist from the inside, I exist, I never choose life, life choose me. I must live, celebrating life, I know myself, and the reason for my existence. My soul is super powerful, in my soul there's fire, colors, life never ceased to exist. My soul is on fire purifying all impurities. In this cycle of life, its' a privilege and honor, just being here, happy to be here, life choose me, and I choose to live. One miracle I won't ever refuse.

LIFE CHOOSE ME

LIKE A NEW BORN BABY, I DIDN'T CHOOSE life, like a new born baby, I didn't choose life, life choose me. Life is determining to reproduce, procreate, circulate, and manifesting itself, anytime, everywhere, any place. From the first hour of my birth here in life, I choose to live. If you have the will you be anything you want to be. My eyes have seen, many things before on this planet earth, all of its beautiful creations, the beginning and end of old conceptions, extinction of species, and other stage of our life existence, life is the funniest. I never choose the day I want to be born, race, place, era, or generation. I was born to live, life. Soar life, I am here to stay in my original state.

LOVE IS FREE

IF YOU DEAL WITH THE DEVIL YOU GOING to get pain, love is free love is, a valuable gift to all those who wisely attain it. Something hypnotic, telepathic, when it happens it's like magic, controlling your feelings. Without love, let them live in darkness if they accept darkness, perfect darkness. Holding on too are, as a drowning man grasping at straws, because they have no love. There's always reasons for love faking love, love is not at fault here, because, put them under a spell, pool them, dismiss them, who so ever take love for granted. What love offers needs no approvals from anyone. Love is a power you share with others, this is what love represents, treasure, precious, passion, harmony, highly recommended. One thing I am guilty of is loving. Be true to love and love will be real to you. Let the whole world know love is free, something you can feel, love is me, love is you. High under its' spell.

THE SPECTRUM

OUR TEACHING IS IN ADEQUATE, TAKING WORDS SYMBOLICALLY is a product of your own circumstances. Those private wild, idle, speculations, like wild fire how quickly they would spread, accept the fact no one is above the spectrum not last, nor least, a human being. As a member of mankind I need clear and precise, answers to every question I may ask. Why commonsense, and natural understanding are not the main ingredient we apply to our intelligence, we are who we are. Accept the fact it's a unification towards a brighter future, time is already ahead of us. Protect the innocence that is out of balance with nature. The pendulum is in motion, actively.

EVERYTHING IS INTERCONNECTED

EVERY ACTION THERE'S A REACTION, DEEP OR HIGH, where there's darkness there's light, darkness, and light, the embodiment of time. What life is worth living for, I discover there are many things that make life a beautiful gift everything is interconnected intellectually designed in life there are many stages, some people approach life on wishes, and dreams, only making life harder than it is, don't let your imagination ever play tricks on you. The pendulum is in motion, actively, negative, and positively, out of balance with nature. Let us sow seeds of survival in order to bear fruits to balance our nation. Make war an unnecessary game on this planet. The whole world would be a much more beautiful place for all the share. We are running out of time.

MANIFESTATION

MANIFESTATION, TIME, MY MIND IS MOVING THROUGH SPACE like light, infinitely. Manifestation, the sun rules by day, and the moon, and stars by night. There's an appointed time for everything, past, present, and future, time is time, it doesn't matter in which direction it flows, you cannot get back time, time belongs to no one. In that moment in time my spiritual being conception was manifested, and in this physical form of entity in which I now exist, meditation time, my mind, like light, is travel though space, and time. Same amount of time, before, here, and forever, and after, it's the same thing. It's the same reason this the same thing. It's the same reason this moment we are sharing is the most important of them all. Manifestation, time, it belongs to no one, we can't get back time, open your mind, meditation, manifestation. Time, time is what we need. It's coming, and going.

VICTORY

THERE'S A LION IN ME I AM ONE who writes history from my point of view, because today defeat will be tomorrow's victory. There's many ways to view history. So many questions. No one answer, no silver bullet. But lift u the past, and put it into the future, and let us see what we make of it. Improvising, recalculating, the position there's many ways, many angles to accomplish the mission today for you, tomorrow for me. Getting the satisfaction of more than I expected, shining like a diamond making it more possible than I actually thought, bring to life a sculptured detail of art, man there's a lion in me.

MAN, A PREDOMINANT SPICES BY WHO'S AUTHORITY

MAN, HE MAN, HAS MADE CLAIMS, SOME MAYBE factual, but occasionally, thinks, and carry out his actions as the most predominant spices. Leaving all others, all life forms to a merger existence, by who's authority? From dust he came with high expectation on his mind all in the name of science, and technology. Bigger, faster, easier, quicker, further, to satisfaction of his needs. Man has all the time in the world to waste. No way of telling, bitter from sweet. The difference from his original stages. Horizontal to vertical. They are chasing insignificantly to the purpose of time, and places. He's above the earth, racing to eternal youth. Age is no more a number of his physical state, only a short length of days after the pleasures then come roses. Adamant, I feel strong about this, form dust he came to this entity, he born, he dies, a living organism in the cycle of life, as a part of time, from dust he came, to dust he shall return a destructive entity.

MAN, O, MAN

MAN, O, MAN, HOW OFTEN HAVE YOU thought up so many inventions, some useful and handy, so many destructive in design. A man is just a man, no color, no class, or race. If this may seem too complicated to you. When the heaven, and earth were created, man became a universal citizen, a member of mankind. Too much rules, and regulation, bureaucracy. Is a big complication, complicating our lives. Exempt immigration, and customs duties you have imposed on the people. No boarder lines, no wire fences, stop building walls, and open the globe, open it up to all who want to come, and go to any country, and be free. Man, O, man, make us walk together, travel the land from coast to coast. Sail the seven seas, and cross the oceans. Everywhere we want to go. Come let's go for a ride, spin, rotate, float, defy gravity fields on a galactic journey outer planetary systems among the stars. Here to continue on our crest for knowledge, and understanding of mankind place in the universe. Man, O, man let's keep moving, moving with a universe expanding with time, interconnecting everything in a continuous cycle, life, death, and beyond man existence.

NO ONE ON THE POOR MAN SIDE

WHY IS THIS HAPPENING, THE POOR MAN HAS no one his side. But on the side of the oppressor is power. Make sure your heart is in the right place, I mean do the right thing and if you don't believe in God, your conscience be your guide. A clear conscience comfortable in your own skin. We maybe a little different the big difference is we all still have to do our best. Don't judge, it won't do us any good, but portray elements of negative energy. It's the golden rule, the same yearning we all share, and value, I can feel, you can feel to, with no mix emotions. Thoughtfulness, love, kindness, compassion, gratefulness, and forgiveness. The same positive attitudes towards life we should display. That is the goodness that nature brings.

THE HEART OF A LION, THE BLOOD RUNS THROUGH OUR LINES COME NOW MY PEOPLE

LET JAH ARISE, AND THE HEATHENS BE SCATTERED, man shall not live by bread alone but by every word that proceed from Jah! They are struggling with the social media black on black, crime destroying the young generation, for what the devils know, he's on the prowl. The Prophets already give us the warning, what more could I say, we got to be strong let us live, get the victory we deserve, let us sow good seeds to reap the purest of the fullness. Of the earth action speaks loader than words, any day, talk is cheap. Too much talk. Let us remember, all our brother, and sister who die in the struggle, may they rest in perfect peace. Be thankful you are alive, everyone deserves a second chance, nothing would make the pain go away anytime soon, unless we trust in each other. No man is an island, they can't back us up against a wall, we will never give up this struggle it must be truly inspiring to one another. Why must we go down with their confusion.

Everything has a purpose.

THE MATERIAL COME, FROM THE SEEN, AND UNSEEN

IT'S SPIRITUAL, THIS FEROCIOUS NATURE LOVE, FORM THE body into the future poetry is uses to my heart.

NEW POSSIBILITIES

MANKIND WE SHOULD BE FOCUSING ON NEW POSSIBILITIES. What are color, shape, or shades, have to do with water yet it is but pure liquid. Life on the earth keep turning around. Darkness into night, east, west, north, south, hot, cold, wet, dry. Negative, and positive, I don't know what on earth is going on why we all can't live together, on a long and short day. Don't let the sun go down, because it isn't it's the earth that is going around, it's an obitual motion, tell who knows when. What a wonderful place, we are already in space, the universe is a living thing. Black, white, yellow, brown. Hi, low, happy, sad, tall, short, fat, thin, up down, right, wrong. We all embrace love. Some like it bitter, some like it sweet, if you are hungry, is time to eat. When you are tired, get some sleep if you are thirsty, water will quench your thirst, water is good, the sun isn't going down. For every one who think the earth is flat.

God is God, God is divine, God is separate he can declare the end from the beginning, and proclaim things not yet done, and then revelation is not sealed, it's revealing, user presumption process of this world.

PRINCESS

MOTHER, BEARER OF GRACE, WOMAN, DAUGHTER, MOTHER OF life. Woman all we ever needed was your love, then, there and now is life. Woman, it is good we already have you. Living is hard, that is what they say. Woman, you have what we need. A big thing, in small step to channel the change in the way which we think. Predicting the future is a very hard thing to do, a woman will love one, and forever will her whole heart. I am with you, woman. I have never found any like you woman in my life time, or before, woman, I need you to stick around. It is rear the trusting kind, it's too hard too fine. She is like the hardest rock, black diamond. Woman, you got an edge on me. Not many had the opportunity to know a woman. We are not going to fine them any better, we desire a woman. You got an edge on me, like crazy squirrels, running around in circles, they did not know what to do. A little bit, or a lot, nothing more, nothing at all you got to do is love her. Forever, real love hurts, fake love is cold. She is a caring one, that bring me numerous happiness. Pretty, woman you got an edge on me.

I don't know how life were created, but if I did, it would be a great opportunity, I see Jah, when I feel like cool breeze blow, he's working hard for me.

MOTHER

YOUR SPIRIT CALM, AND TENDERLY, YOU TOOK ME under your wings. You shared with me what life is truly worth living for in every aspect of my world you made your point clear, so far you have no intention of going anywhere. In many critical moments in my life, symmetrically fine turning my life, willing to go infinite distance, closely I will be cherishing all those moment, fortunate to share those experience, truly grateful. In body, mind, and spirit, live a great live that your soul escape deprivation, and poverty, the shallow, dark shadows, showed at your acts of kindness. This state of mind of yours has followed you, giving you good health, with fortune all your days of our life. It all has been transparent through the good, and bad of life. I woke up this morning, suddenly to this mission, to proclaim this special day of the year to you. Every day is a most special one, so there's no reason to discriminate. As one day pass another return, consecutively. My dear mother, from me to you, this day I dedicate my infinite love, loving you always, you are not getting any younger, black hair are now turning gray, but keep on moving on with life as you feel. However, this day I could never forget, every day I exist mom, from me to you, have a happy mother.

TRICK IS A TRICK

FREEDOM IS A DESERVING, BASIC, FUNDAMENTAL HUMAN RIGHT to every living soul, but justice would not be served, but reserve, happiness could never be achieved in a state where only a few will seldom share, black man where is your pride as living examples, what about your sweet heritage? What they teach us is not sufficient, inefficient, useless to our future. You give us the books enslaving the mental weak. A trick is a trick, saying we have got any soul, trick my fore parent, call us niggers, worthless, worse than anything I would of ever accepted, to a subhuman existence, it's written in history, if something was to go wrong it would, Murphy's law, it's sure to take effect, creating a fire in the end. My generation is crying out for drastic change, east, west, north, and south, return to the cycle of life. The one reason, the only purpose I exist her for, and that would be to live, equal to all on this globe, all life, yesterday, today, and tomorrow. These are the cause of the problems. You punish me for my intelligence, and great accomplishments, pressing me for the bad. Dead ends, mental stress, racism, discrimination and hate, only hurts our integrity and credibility. Why these thing follows us for no reason, are you trying to cheat us, we want to be freed, no equal opportunity, as minorities. Our self-worth, and contribution must count, immensely significant, ignoring our excellence. Because love shines bright, our light that guides our treasure soul, keeping us in existence.

NEVER TO SOON OR TO LATE

WHEN IT RAINS I POURS, THERE'S NO ANSWERS to the number of troubles I have to face, and I don't know if it would ever change. There's a place you could always fine answers. When you stop and search, deep within yourself. I guess you haven't notice, I guess you haven't heard, tomorrow is just another day. Living in the moment there's no time as the present. Forgive, judge no one, sorry is essential, who is to be blame, so stop your negative thinking, and think positive, consciously making your choices at the end of the day. There's an unseen force in the universe, I know it keeps me grounded, in my world that keep turning around, can you feel it, I can feel it, everything is happen very fast all at once. Like a strange dream to my mind between our desires and broken promises. Love one abandon by greed, at the same time another one died, another one is born, such things are not to sane, not unusual they were here before, young here today, gone tomorrow, it's a screwed up world, I feel like just floating away to elevate life challenges, no easy feat, I am a man, and not a child. Life is what you make it, never to soon or too late. And tomorrow is another day. There will be an answer if you just let it be, what it will be.

GREAT AFRICA

AFRICA, MY SOUL BELONGS TO YOU, form the time the universe, and creation, great ancient land, civilization of my ancestors who contributed rich colorful culture to mankind. Africa, and African has embraced their liberty for thousands of years on this planet earth. With its mysterious effect in the conversation the continent, the whole land scape, from Timbuktu to Egypt and Ethiopia. The land is enormously self-sufficient, rich in minerals, and natural resources. Africa could feed its people throughout their whole life time, one of the greatest continents. Their human spirit has triumph by far, my people has endured by their unquestionable skill, and talent, the evidence is self-explanatory to that fact, Africa, never needed any favor from outside help given the abundance by creation and nature's gifts. There's no telling the level of society we could achieve. Fine arts, sculpture, and giant monuments, with the evidence warranty culminating life of the black man.

WEARY OF CONVICTION

MY SOUL GROWS WEARILY OF CONVICTIONS, WHO WILL care for the welfare of my family my body resistance is voluntary depriving itself of all substances, prepare for the soles of despair, and uncertainty. Struggling to my bills, cloth myself, and fine food to put on my table. A victim of society, trying to legitimately analyze what was transpiring here before me, how did I find myself in this tragedy. I fund no mental scope of escaping. Then a deep, stern voice said to me, once you receive this visitation, its' your invitation to stay, not to leave, internally I feel my bowels squeeze, my bone mas decreased, my knees was failing my body right. About to faint, courage turned into negative energy, projecting volts of fear. Now I am tired, to turn to a trapped imagination turn again to realistic manna. Vision the abyss surround by darkness with no capacity to convey any clear thoughts. In solitude I still found myself in a sense of uncertainty. Could anything set this mind of mine at ease. Maybe some uninterrupted moments would be the best part of the coming years ahead.

WATER, NO AGUA?

EYES BEHIND THE WATER FALL. TEARS RUNNING DOWN the face of the mountain. The sky is in a beautiful glaze catching the remaining light of the evening sun. rivers run cold, yet steaming as they flow through the seven colors of my thoughts. Red, orange, yellow, green, blue, indigo, violet, tinge. My thoughts seem to drift away on life without these two elements, hydrogen, and oxygen, is life without the falling rain. Lush valleys, meadows, and plains. If you want to cook, clean, or shower, no water, thirst, and dehydration. Water is a form of dense liquid in the form of ice no color, atoms vaporize into the atmosphere, too repair again in the form as rain. Liquid in its original state taking, any form, any shape. The one element most essential to every living thing that ever live, and, breathes. Imagine one day you woke up and there's no water, no one drops to be found, in the rivers, springs, lakes, seas, and oceans. Open your eyes, we should be in an alarm concerning water conservation or one day you may open you tap and only thing you get was thin air. No water, anywhere. This is water at sub 0-degree temperature, glacial melting at the Artic Poles.

FATHERLESS CHILDREN

THIS IS THE SONGS OF THE FATHERLESS CHILDREN a poem of the times. What is the worse to expect, rebuked, rejected, abandon, and scorned? By a system, confusion in this song, my own government want to see me dead, take my life away. My life had no worth to them, no value, reduced to a subhuman existence. This is my poem, a song of the revolutionary spirit. I found a way to discover knowledge to eliminate the negativities and threats. I don't want to walk in humiliation, as a black man I am a living example. Smart, driven by natural wits, looking up, not down, positive in every action I take, always moving forward, not backward. Free in this song, a poem of love, and reality, drinking from the fountain of life. There comes a time to reflect on being a better person. I know I won't be in vain, a brand new me has become my life style, gaining visions of life throughout eternity, independent of this world. Others happiness is just as important as my happiness, the root to this success is loving each other, love must shine, fresh as the spring time.

BLACK, AND POOR IN THE GHETTOS

THERE'S SOMETHING SO MANY OF US HAS DONE in this life before, whether we were guilty or innocent, born black, and poor in the ghettoes. The system is deadly terrors, the system detrimental murder by psychological war fare, like they forget we are poor people, labeling us as criminals, locking us up in jail, prisons, even though we are trying to do our very best. Trying very hard to hold on to our faiths. Their shoes, and ties they wear are outrageously more expensive than our food rent, and bills. We have nothing at all to call our own. I was born this way am no different, everything is on go slow, suffering is all we know in our world. It doesn't matter how hard you try every day is the same pattern over, and over again, northing seems to change this program. For the weary mind looking for any new experience, one-way is to hell holds all the challenges to drive the sane, insane. The only element to cope with this environment making any difference is our will to live, survive the days that turn into years passing by not in unawareness of how long we have been down. The time is getting shorter, many of us is dying, some so innocent for no reason, no cause whatsoever at all. Who ever thought it would be like this? Who say life was fare, life was nice, stand up, and show your hand up high.

MAN BY NATURE

MAN BY NATURE HAVE HIS DOUBTS, FEARS, CONVICTIONS, love, and a kind personality. Functioning in a society, fighting for a cause in the human condition, living under a common experience. Myself today must relate to myself of yesterday, and must relate to myself if yesterday, and likely as myself tomorrow in a unique sense on the grounds of finding myself as a unique individual. My values, principles, and integrity. These vision are sure base on the levels of my thoughts, visions straight from my heart. I ask what can I do for you, with the capabilities, and skills was acquired. I am able to transcend by my different action I lay no heavy burden on you, no rules but the spiritual wellbeing of a people is a human reality, know it is quite possible to learn working together to develop all of mankind, this would be an important moral contribution. But it is unacceptable in every sense for ignorance, and a nasty attitude, there's no excuse. This is a very crucial point, and time of our lives. Poor teaching is a guarantee that too late, too little, would be done to our behavior and, manners only leaning little of ourselves.

THE CYCLE OF NATURE'S WAY

LIFE IS A CYCLE, HOW DOES IT KEEPS on turning I can't tell, I cannot explain. I can't believe what is happening today. Human suffering, and pain at its highest level, only a few on top is going to win, and the poor got to pay. Spiritually and clinically out of balance with the cycle of and nature of things, a very serious problem. Like an object in motion, am on my way to destiny, on my mission to fine the purpose I was meant to fulfill. When I arrive I know it's going to be grate, always on my heels, looking up, not down. The journey is just as import as the destiny, searching for the things which comes from within my fiery soul. Ditching wicked, society. Right now, this minute, today. It's a troubled world we are living inn; there's no sort of change life is like a journey that never end. It's not an easy road. Everyone is unique in their own individual way, ones with exceptional talent and skill, has the tools to prove who they truly are. Speak the truth, always, just let it be. Shine your light from the mountain top for the whole wide trouble world could see.

JOHN SAW A DOOR IN HEAVEN, AND HE SAW A THRONE

EVERYTHING ON ME UNAWARE, IS COMMON BY THE one who sets on the throne. Listen to the sound, no one else come here, this sound, no one else could learn this sound, no one else but the righteous, redeem, understand it. No one else could sing this sound. My song cools the mind downs my song, it most rewarding. Listen, no one else could, hear, learn, and understand the ups, and downs, it's righteous, redeeming, rewarding. My song is a cool song too sing. My song is sweet. The fallen the innocent, and burn our homes, John saw a door open in heaven, and he saw a throne, everything in the universe, is controlled by the one who sits on the throne, there's a reason they can't touch my soul it's love, and comforting, it doesn't move, like the only star in the sky, the north star just would, it make you very happy.

IN THE ABSENCE OF A DAD

IN THE ABSENCE OF A DAD, GOD BE my witness. It's a rough ocean, high seas, hide tides. But it doesn't matter what the tide may bring in, one way or the other I had to make a change. Clean up this mess, help myself, overcome the stress or be a slave to my insecurities. The rest of my days. In the absence of a dad, I was heading down a dead-end street, going nowhere dangerously fast, trying to make my mark. No role model, no hero's no one cheered to make me feel proud. In a wild state of mind. It was bad things, mentally stress, more problem for a single parent mom. Physically drained, were only half the story of my life many thoughts flowed through my head life didn't seems to worth anything to me all, many personal experience, constantly, contemplating where to begin. My plans were not going to be one that include failure. Adamantly I must ultimately win. Slow down the paste but by bit, be a little more patient, making small steps. Visualizing the big picture. Anything can happen, don't tell me it's impossible, finding new path already laid down. I could make up, down, crooked, straight, elevating my mind to nature's plan, to every action there's a reaction. Tears today but joy comes in the morning. Sunshine, and the world a more colorful place. I will take the good with the bad, one way or the other. I have to make a change, clean up the mess, help myself, overcome this life, in the absence of a dad, God be my witness.

LIVING IS NOT EASY, THERE'S ALWAYS A TRADE of back too square one, and you don't have anything to show for you efforts but your courage. It's an important thing. I see you questioning your ability to succeed. You have to decide if you are ready for a new chapter, are you certain you are really, ready, with better results.

You are trying, trying too hard to fit in, when you should be outstanding many time you though it was all positive. Connections is a much bigger thing. We always coming second place, there's a bigger picture, can't you see it, willingly, struggling with all your desires from the bottom we have become out right, rivals.

BLESS, THIS DAY I WAS BORN

WHAT AM I LIVING FOR? THIS COULD NEVER be all too my existence from manifestation of this beautiful life. When did I all began? Where do I go from here? What decision do I make in life? One day, one life, whether we live or die, one day I was granted life, bless that day.

One day too live, one day too die. It's not self-serving. A thousand year with God is like one-day pass. Water takes on any form, any shape. Bless my life is connected too, the, earthy, sun, moon, and stars. I feel like jumping, I really feel like jumping, and touch the clear blue skies, happiness is the ultimate high. Teach the world the truth.

I am the only one who could make me feel good, feel the happiest. I love sincerity, because it's lovely one thing or the other. Don't leave u to someone else to do what you always do for yourself.

In harmony with light, solar, atomic, energy. It's time to lift yourself up. The trade winds are blowing, coming, and going as they please. Make my day resilient in every way, with expectation. Constantly improving on the levels of my life, I can't be measured, or be compromised.

I could do the greatest things imaginable, I could adopt to my environment. Confident, deeply rooted stretching my imagination for my mind, for light from the sky for a thousand generation.

LIFE IS A MYSTERY

BIRTH IS A MYSTERY, DEATH IS A MYSTERY, life is a mystery. No one knows what tomorrow may bring. One thing we all desire, is too live a good life. But some are poor, some are rich, some healthy, some sick.

Life is like a forest in the winter time, form a distance it looks complicated, until you set your minds on the right trail. Grab your paper, and your pen. Today don't look nothing like yesterday.

You can't tell the whole story from a male or female point of view. One life opens many doors through different experience. The entire story cannot be detail the turmoil could never be told by words which has be loss.

What is the essence of, shame, pleasure, and pain? Without any information, pieces of the puzzle seem to be out of place. Hunger, with no food to eat. You try to resist when hunger talk to the gut, the desire is an urgent need for food.

Money, the rich have it all, it not everyone could afford to get it, and they still want more. The same, today, and forever more. Love, ready to learn from the novel that we read, we must really care all about love. Eventually, it will follow us, watching us place the fool, love will lead, reflecting the light within. Like a force if energy. Love is never done in weakness should never be mistaken, form kindness. Love tell.

INTELLECT

THEY DON'T WANT US TO BE TOO INTELLECTUAL, but battles are won before they even begin. Grab me a pen, and paper. The pen is mightier than the gun. Think about the past, and the journey has just begun. Think about life, and the things you know we need to change.

Experience has brought us through some of the roughest times. Put your mind on the future. Life is one road, choose the life you desire to live. Who can you depend on. So far, you made too this present day. Clear your mind, entertain good thoughts, and nothing could hold you back.

Everything is within your reach, let's go to the beginning, and your place in creation, and sure no one had any control. The universe was in a hot dense state, and this is how it turn out today. Evolution, is such a controversial, concept of topic. How could you come from agree, who could believe he came from primates.

I am hyperventilating, they better fine me a new theory. A woman was created to be a companion too man; too replenish, and multiply the earth. It takes nothing too love, it take a lot to be a man. But you were born a man there's a lot of information relevant to this case.

The name of God burns through the hearty of evil doers. I shall serve the Lord, pass it on to the children, not selective, but respected. The passion must live on in each other. Let our true purpose for being here be revealed.

www.ingramcontent.com/pod-product-compliance
Lightning Source LLC
Chambersburg PA
CBHW021644120626
46545CB00002B/703